D0089034

"*Brandraising* is a timely, critically important contribution for all nonprofits. As 'competition' intensifies, resources dwindle, and senior executives are drawn to react in short-term crisis mode, it becomes even more vital that external (and internal!) communications stay as strategic as possible. The ultimate perception of 'brand' will be the extent to which the audience clearly understands the organization's vision, and Sarah Durham gets this ironclad principle. With step-by-step sage guidance, *Brandraising* should be a dog-eared resource for perceptive chief executives in the sector."

—Mark Lipton, consultant on nonprofit board strategy and professor of management, Milano: The New School for Management and Urban Policy

"*Brandraising* is a must-read for any organization operating in the noisy and crowded nonprofit arena today. Sarah Durham 'flips the switch' on our understanding of a holistic communications strategy. Like the architecture of the planning and implementation she encourages, the architecture of this book delivers a clear and smart message. Finally, in one volume we can find the structure and the techniques any institution can use to place itself above the din."

—Nancy Schwartz Sternoff, director, Dobkin Family Foundation

"Sarah Durham presents her considerable expertise with a smart combination of authority and accessibility that makes *Brandraising* a must-read for fundraisers and nonprofit communications and marketing staff—no matter how long they've been in the business or the size and mission of their organizations. The book's hip yet down-to-earth tone is a perfect reflection of Sarah herself, as is its finely balanced respect for traditional strategies with a serious, forward-looking nod to new technologies."

—Margaret Battistelli, editor-in-chief, *Fundraising Success*

"If you lead a nonprofit organization and you want to be successful, you better read this book—right now! In today's highly fragmented and fast-moving world, it is important for an organization to have a strong brand. Scratch that—it's necessary, critical, obligatory, unavoidable. Nonprofit organizations must demonstrate their vision, mission, values, objectives, positioning, and personality in every aspect of their work. If they don't, their audience won't engage, their issues won't resonate, and they will fail. Creating that strong brand is no easy task. Navigating the process of building and maintaining brand can be frustrating and exhausting. Sarah Durham understands that. She has spent her life helping nonprofit organizations build strong brands and communicate successfully. And now she has written a book that provides clear guidelines, valuable lessons, and powerful examples that nonprofit organizations can use to build their brand and succeed in their work."

—**Brian Reich, coauthor,** *Media Rules: Mastering Today's Technology to Connect With and Keep Your Audience*

"In today's highly competitive nonprofit sector, creating an effective brand is essential. *Brandraising* tells you how to do it right! It should be required reading by today's executive director, development director, communications director, or other nonprofit professional."

—**Cheryl A. Clarke, consultant and author of** *Storytelling for Grantseekers* **and** *Grant Proposal Makeover*

"During these uncertain economic times, when organizations' staffs are required to do more with much less, while meeting an ever growing need, *Brandraising* is a must-read for nonprofit professionals looking to help their organizations thrive or even just survive. Although nonprofits generally spend time on strategic planning, Sarah Durham brings home the point that executing the strategies is an entirely different set of tasks. *Brandraising* illustrates how strategically planned and executed tactics in branding, communications, and fundraising are critical ingredients for solvent and successful nonprofit organizations."

—**Nicci Noble, president, Noble Services**

Brandraising

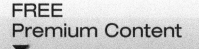

FREE Premium Content ▼	JOSSEY-BASS™ An Imprint of ⊛WILEY
This book includes premium content that can be accessed from our Web site when you register at **www.josseybass.com/go/sarahdurham** using the password *professional*.	

Brand^{raising}

HOW NONPROFITS RAISE VISIBILITY AND MONEY THROUGH SMART COMMUNICATIONS

Sarah Durham

JOSSEY-BASS
A Wiley Imprint
www.josseybass.com

Published by Jossey-Bass
A Wiley Imprint
989 Market Street, San Francisco, CA 94103-1741—www.josseybass.com

Jossey-Bass books and products are available through most bookstores. To contact Jossey-Bass directly call our Customer Care Department within the U.S. at 800-956-7739, outside the U.S. at 317-572-3986, or fax 317-572-4002.

Jossey-Bass also publishes its books in a variety of electronic formats. Some content that appears in print may not be available in electronic books.

Cataloging-in-Publication Data on file with the Library of Congress.

ISBN-13: 978-0-470-52753-5

Printed in the United States of America

FIRST EDITION
HB Printing   10 9 8 7 6 5

CONTENTS

For my family

Brandraising

CHAPTER 1

Brandraising

During the fall of 2008, right in the middle of the financial market's collapse, I facilitated a panel on branding at an event called "Meet the Grantmakers," organized by the Support Center for Nonprofit Management. Throughout the morning, several officers of large corporate foundations talked about how their foundations' endowments had plummeted, leading to fewer grants and less money awarded to nonprofits. These grantmakers stressed that the competition for available grants was going to be tougher than ever. Organizations applying would have to distinguish themselves by communicating clearly and demonstrating their value distinctively. By the time my afternoon panel on branding began, the big question on everyone's mind seemed to be, *How can we demonstrate our value and uniqueness with our limited staff, budget, and experience in the area of communications?*

Let's face it: nonprofits arrived very late at the marketing party. Back in 1994, when I started working with nonprofits, words like *branding*, *marketing*, and *messaging* were often misunderstood, ignored, or treated as dirty words. Perhaps this was because *marketing* is a term most often associated with selling, and the idea of having to sell a nonprofit's benefits (to donors or clients, for example) felt strange.

Although development is a powerful department in most nonprofit organizations, it often functions independently from the program or advocacy departments. Each department usually produces its own materials, with no coordination or oversight, with the result that a direct-mail appeal, for example, doesn't relate to what's on the organization's Web site or what's in its overview brochure or even what's on the sign posted in the lobby.

In the for-profit world, corporations place a high value on marketing. Branding is a line item in any start-up's budget, and communications-focused staff people (usually with "marketing" titles) are among the first to be hired. In contrast, new nonprofits rarely provide budgeting or staffing for communications. Instead, all resources are invested in launching programs, and communications evolve on an ad hoc basis. Scrappy and hard-working staff members at new nonprofits manage with whatever they've got as they seek out funding, attract clients, and establish other relationships.

But in the past few years the conversation has shifted as nonprofits of all sizes see more and more examples of how branding and marketing build valuable relationships with donors, clients, and other key constituents. Larger nonprofits (typically those with annual budgets of $5 million or more) invest in communications as a separate department, and fundraisers increasingly embrace the notion that they are marketers. Even the term *branding* is now commonly used.

Whether the economy is good or bad, whether the competition for funding is tough or not, and whether they're small or large, organizations must communicate every day. Staff members send e-mail blasts, hold events, update Web sites, solicit donors, tweet, create newsletters, and more. Most do so with little or no centralization, coordination, time, training, budget, or support. Without realizing it, many organizations end up putting the cart before the horse, usually because they lack a clear framework for communications strategy, decision making, and execution. Nonprofits redo their Web site in the middle of strategic planning, for example. It's like trying to install a window before you've built the wall.

Chapter Two, "Principles of Effective Communications," takes a closer look at the value of communicating more deliberately and at some of the obstacles that make that particularly hard to do in today's workplace.

What "Brandraising" Means

Cattle ranchers branded their livestock with the symbols of their ranch to distinguish them from other ranchers' stock. Many people today still associate the word *brand* with a symbol—usually a logo. Some people think it also includes colors, messaging, and other elements that distinguish an organization. Although those associations are valuable, they lack a connection to an organization's mission and vision or to its impact, the things that all organizations are ultimately about.

For most nonprofits, raising money and increasing visibility are the primary reasons to communicate. *Brandraising* is the process of developing a clear, cohesive organizational identity and communications system that supports these goals and makes it easier to express the organization's mission effectively and consistently.

In centuries past, communities came together and worked collaboratively to assemble barns, arguably the most important structure on a farm. Working as a well-choreographed team, all the members of the community played a role in planning, directing, constructing, or supporting the assembly of the barn. When the barn was finished, a single cohesive structure stood, providing shelter for the farm's animals, tools, and supplies.

Brandraising, like barn raising, involves everyone in your nonprofit's community—board members and staff leaders, volunteers, program staff, and perhaps donors and funders. Everyone plays a role in the development of effective communications.

Throughout this book the term *brandraising* is used to describe the process of building a strong framework for communicating. The elements involved in brandraising and their connections to each other are outlined at the beginning of Chapter Three, "Overview of Brandraising," and then defined and explored in greater detail in the four chapters that follow.

If you work at a nonprofit and have little or no background in communications, this book should help you manage any branding or communications-related work more effectively. If you are a more experienced nonprofit professional grappling with the rise of social media and other unexpected changes in the communications landscape, it should help you stay current.

Measuring the Value of Communications

In a business that sells widgets, the ROI (return on investment) is measured by profit.

But in the nonprofit world, the impact of communications is measured in terms of the ability of those communications to support and advance the mission. More specifically, it is measured by

- *Impact on income.* Ask yourself: Did the communications investment help us build successful relationships with the individuals, corporations, foundations, or governmental agencies that support our organization financially? Did it increase donations or attract new donors? This impact is particularly critical during an economic downturn.
- *Impact on programs.* Ask yourself: Did the communications investment help us reach the right people for our programs, keep them engaged, and truly work toward achieving our objectives and mission?
- *Impact on advocacy.* Ask yourself: Did the communications investment help us effectively influence legislation, change perceptions around issues, and position our organization as the leading go-to resource in its field?

Most nonprofits communicate in order to

- Raise money (*fundraising*).
- Reach the right audiences for their programs (sometimes called *outreach*).
- Establish their leadership position around their core issues (*advocacy*).

Some organizations experience significant overlap among their fundraising, program, and advocacy audiences (illustrated in Figure 1.1). For instance, a symphony's donors are also subscribers to its programs and might also be community leaders who help to shape the group's reputation in the area. Conversely, some groups have very disparate audiences, with little overlap. For example, an agency may be reliant on funding from foundations, have

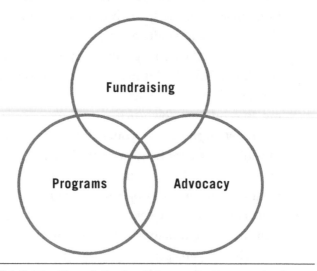

FIGURE 1.1 The Shared Goals of Nonprofit Communications

programs that work with people who are homeless, and lobby politicians for change that will benefit its clients (for instance, affordable housing).

In a for-profit organization, transactions are simpler. A customer buys a product or service and pays for it. Happy customers often lead to a profitable business. But in a nonprofit, this can be far from the case; even an extremely successful program will close its doors if funding dries up.

The true value of communications is measured through income generated, programs that achieve their stated goals, and other tangible results. Branding is certainly not a panacea. If a nonprofit organization is ineffective, corrupt, or has lost its way, good communications might delay but will not stop its collapse. But in my experience, most organizations are full of extremely hard-working people doing exceptionally good work. The principles of effective communications and brandraising strategy covered in the following chapters will maximize such organizations' effectiveness.

In Summary

- Unlike for-profits, nonprofit organizations usually fail to allocate resources for marketing or communications in their early years. Often, staffing and budgeting for communications doesn't happen until years into an organization's existence, which can present challenges.
- Increasingly, nonprofit leaders are seeing the value of marketing, branding, and communications.

- Brandraising is the process of developing a clear and cohesive organizational identity and communications system that supports the organization's mission.
- Nonprofits typically communicate for three purposes: to raise money, to reach audiences for programs (outreach), and to advocate (with legislators, the media, or within a community).

CHAPTER 2

Principles of Effective Communications

Traditionally, for-profit companies have integrated marketing and communications *best practices* into their day-to-day activities much more successfully and effectively than nonprofits have. Why is that?

Young nonprofits find it much harder than their for-profit counterparts do to build in communications budgets, staff, and infrastructure from the start. Perhaps that's because nonprofits are inherently more complicated, with their varied levels of leadership, diverse audiences, and complex ways of generating income. Launching themselves with a focus on mission and programs is, perhaps, challenging enough.

In 2008, Big Duck (my communications company, which works exclusively with nonprofits) conducted an informal, online survey of nonprofits to identify the things that made it hard for them to communicate. The Barriers to Effective Communications survey highlighted three resource shortages as the greatest communications obstacles non-profit professionals experience:

- Not having the time to develop or implement a proper communications strategy (27.8 percent)
- Not having the budget to implement what they want to do (21.7 percent)
- Not having communications expertise within the organization (9.1 percent)

Nonprofits' lack of time, money, and expertise for communications didn't surprise us at Big Duck. In fact, these were the barriers we expected to find. But as we dug deeper, a few other interesting barriers revealed themselves. Mostly, they centered around a lack of understanding of the basic principles of effective communications. So before diving into an overview of brandraising in Chapter Three, this discussion will examine the principles of effective communications and the obstacles that prevent nonprofits from applying them.

Seeing the Long View

The Appalachian Trail, at 2,175 miles, is the nation's longest marked footpath. It touches fourteen states between Georgia, its southernmost point, and Maine, where its northern end lies. In a typical year over a thousand people set out to Thru-Hike the Appalachian Trail. Most will travel from south to north, starting in early March or April and finishing before the northern end of the trail closes to overnight hikers in mid-October. Typically, fewer than three hundred people will make it.

Supplies, including water, are heavy to carry, so advance planning is necessary to figure out where they will be acquired. Even figuring out what sort of food will be easiest to carry, prepare, and digest while on the trail requires planning. From a distance, it may sound like a nice vacation to take six months off from work to hike and camp. But completing the Thru-Hike requires ample preparation: being in good condition for hiking and carrying a heavy pack, mapping out supply acquisitions, even enlisting family members to mail packages prepared in advance on specific dates to post offices near the trail.

Managing communications—indeed, managing an organization—is similar. At the beginning a founder's passion and focus feels like enough to make it all happen. Founders often single-handedly do the work of many, moving mountains along the way. Most never pause to anticipate what growing the organization may require or to consider sustainability. Who can say what may come up? What extreme measures may be taken? What resources will be most important to help the organization thrive?

Taking the long view organizationally requires both planning and agility. When leaders and staff act with the future in mind, systems can be built to help the nonprofit weather challenges.

Yet many organizations manage communications and other areas myopically, with only the short term in mind. Even though they may spend time planning where they would like their programs and services to be in the future, they rarely consider how they would like donors, clients, policymakers, or other key constituents to perceive them in the longer term. Does your nonprofit take a long or short view of communications? Compare the views displayed in Table 2.1.

Successful direct-mail programs are a good example of taking the long view. Organizations that make money on these programs do it over the long run; they know that even though an individual appeal to prospects may not be very profitable, the new donors it brings to the organization will deliver over time.

Working Reactively

Does your organization have a communications calendar that it uses to plan when e-mails, mailings, newsletters, invitations, and other pieces will drop? Are you planning and starting these communications well in advance, or are you producing them at the last minute and scrambling to get them done?

Taking the short view instead of budgeting and building communications for the long haul tends to create a culture of working *reactively*—not *proactively*.

A reinventing of the wheel happens when staff end up working reactively. Text is written from scratch because there is no preexisting boilerplate, set of key messages, or style guide to inform copywriting. New designs bear little resemblance to other organizational materials. The result is a hodgepodge of communications sending out mixed signals. The first step in avoiding this confusion is to assemble a detailed calendar showing when all projects should begin and end—with rounds of back-and-forth planned between the beginning and end of each project—and then stick to this schedule.

TABLE 2.1 Which View Does Your Organization Take?

Short View	Long View
Has no budget for communications; projects are done ad hoc.	Budgets annually for ongoing communications.
Postpones overhauling important communications (brand, Web site, and so forth) until the situation becomes a crisis, then often makes compromises in the development due to limited budget or time to complete it.	Anticipates big expenses in advance (for instance, a new Web site), and seeks funding for them proactively.
Has no formal or written guidelines for maintaining identity and little clarity about who's responsible. Typically, there are no defined key messages.	Has developed a clear visual identity and a messaging platform; these elements are institutionalized in a style guide, staff manual, or other document.
Has developed its visual identity and messaging informally and subjectively.	Has developed its visual identity and messaging platform strategically, with a clear link to the organization's vision and mission. In older organizations, any shifts in the brand occur after strategic planning, to make sure brand and plans are closely linked.
Dives into using new tools (such as social media) or big projects without connecting these projects to other initiatives strategically. As a result, projects short-circuit or must be overhauled sooner than expected.	Doesn't undertake a new communications project (for instance, launching a Facebook group or other social media forum) until it's clear who the audience is, what the project will require of staff, and what the project's purpose is.

Accidental Branding

Most organizations begin with great ideas and limited resources. As a nonprofit develops, it will immediately start communicating with external audiences like clients and funders. Within its first three years an organization is likely to

- Come up with a name for itself and perhaps a tagline too.
- Create a logo.
- Create letterhead and other stationery items.
- Create flyers, brochures, and Web sites and other tools to reach people who might participate in its programs, collaborate as partners, or make donations.
- Spread the word—through written, spoken, or viral correspondence, forming a buzz or reputation.
- Pick a spokesperson or chief communicator by default, rather than deliberately: this person generally writes and edits important correspondence, speaks about the organization regularly, and okays any materials that are developed. (Often, he or she is the executive director or development director.)

In a new nonprofit organization it's rare for staff to have the resources (time and money) to hire professionals to develop and market the organization's brand. Although corporations might easily spend $250,000 or more when rebranding, nonprofits typically budget a small fraction of that amount, if anything at all. Instead, they address these elements on the fly, taking a short-term view of getting them quickly and affordably so they can move on to programs and operations issues.

Developing a name, logo, or other communications element on the fly isn't always a bad thing. Many organizations find that aspects of the resulting accidental brand work well, much to their own surprise. Later, though, the accidental brand approach will typically begin to fail during a period of significant growth or change, when it becomes clear that this isn't an optimal way to communicate.

During these times, staff people say such things as, "We're trying to build a new base of support from major donors (or corporations), and I don't feel our current brand represents us well. I'm worried funders won't think we're worth a large investment." Or, "I don't feel proud of our logo and other visuals; if we're going to invest in our first expensive annual report [or Web site], I want to do it right, so everything reflects our excellent work." Or, "Our current name seems confusing or misleading when you consider our current programs. As we invest in an outreach campaign for our new program, I want it all to make more sense so new audiences who hear about us will form the right impressions."

Completing a checklist like the following can tell you whether your nonprofit's brand is accidental and it can spark productive discussion about your organization's communications. (*Yes* answers indicate accidental branding.)

☐ Our logo and other graphic elements weren't designed by a professional or well-trained designer.
☐ Our brochures, Web sites, and other communications tools are developed by a variety of people and

they have no continuity: they don't relate to each other or present a cohesive image of what we do.

☐ Every time we write something for external audiences, we start from scratch: we don't use predefined messages or language to ensure consistency in our voice.

☐ Our materials and the brand elements in them have a generic quality that doesn't capture our unique vision and mission: they could be used by other organizations with similar missions.

Monitoring the Landscape

Nonprofit staff with a long-range view regularly monitor what other peer organizations are doing, how they communicate, what results they are getting, and more. Reporting these findings at senior staff or board meetings can benefit an organization in many areas. First, this information builds a sense of context that helps leaders see how their nonprofit stacks up among competing groups. It also highlights areas where the organization is way ahead—or way behind. Because peer organizations may be courting some of the same donors, clients, or policymakers, this information can inform communications with these supporters. For example, sharing positive findings in the larger context of the community can be highly motivating to an invested supporter who wants to see the nonprofit succeed.

Managing Information Saturation

Reaching out to people used to involve activities like getting stamps, sealing envelopes, and waiting days for a reply. Ten or more years ago, it wasn't too hard to imagine that a letter or phone call would be received by someone who might actually pay attention to it. After all, life moved at a slower pace back then and the number of communications we received each day was lower because each one took more effort to produce.

But wow, have times changed. Here are a few statistics that might blow your mind:

- A 2008 survey found that 23 percent of all mobile phone users in the United States (or 58 million users) had been exposed to advertising on their phones in the past thirty days (Loechner, 2008).
- The average American home has the TV on for about 7 hours a day, and "actual viewing is estimated at 4.5 daily hours per adult." When radio, newspapers, and other traditional media are factored in, the average American adult is estimated to spend 6.43 hours each day paying attention to media. (That's more hours than many Americans sleep each night.) (Mayer, n.d.).
- A 2006 survey found that 147 million U.S. adults were Internet users: that's approximately 71 percent of all Americans. Even older adults were well represented: 26 percent of Americans aged seventy to seventy-five were online, and 17 percent of Americans aged seventy-six or older were online too (Madden, 2006).
- By January of 2009, Facebook had over 68,500,000 unique visitors visiting 1,191,373,339 times each month (Kazeniac, 2009).

Need some information or feel curious about something? You *Google* it. You might even send *InMail* to your

LinkedIn professional network, *post* to an interest-specific listserv, or *message* via another social network, such as Facebook. We now have many more ways we can reach out to each other, and these channels are bombarding each of us with information we need to process and respond to.

How are we dealing with all this information? Half of the individuals who completed Big Duck's 2008 Barriers to Effective Communications survey doubted that they had effective tools for managing the information and projects they were handling.

Reinforcing the Big Idea

How many pieces of information have you received from nonprofits in the past week? How carefully did you read them? How much thought did you give to them?

Most people receive 3,000 to 5,000 marketing messages per day from both nonprofits and for-profits. We're all being bombarded with messages, and we're ignoring much of what comes our way daily. Imagine what it must be like to be a philanthropist who receives dozens (if not hundreds) of event invitations, letters of inquiry, and requests for meetings or support. It's no wonder that many major philanthropists have staff acting as their gatekeepers and managing their correspondence.

When you produce these materials, your sense of these items' importance is exponentially greater than the importance they will have to the people who will receive them. Because you are close to this work, it can be hard to remember that others may be less engaged or familiar with your organization's mission or programs. Being clear about the one big idea you hope to communicate, and reinforcing it in every headline, story, or design element, can help you penetrate the noise.

When you look at it from this point of view, the world is a noisy place, and your organization might have to shout a bit—certainly, speak very clearly and consistently—to get its messages across.

Communicating on Their Terms, Not Yours

In this increasingly noisy, information-saturated world, it's harder than ever to get the attention of the individuals your organization must reach. But many organizations add an additional obstacle by communicating about themselves in *me, me, me* terms that feel irrelevant for many of the individuals they're hoping to reach and engage. Instead of telling them why your organization is so great, start by understanding who they are and how they'll benefit from supporting your work. Make the case on their terms, not yours. This is the fundamental principle of *audience-centric communications*, which will be referred to throughout this book.

Looking Through Your Audience's Eyes

Getting your distracted, hard-to-reach audience to pay attention is challenge enough when you've got a multimillion-dollar advertising budget, or so the pages of *Advertising Age* magazine tell us. But what if you've got no budget for communications at all? Then the stakes get even higher.

When your organization plans to produce a newsletter, send out an announcement, or blast an e-mail, do you start by recalling how busy your audiences are and thinking about how and what they might like to hear from you? Are you reaching them in the channels they prefer to use for communication? Is your copy written in a style and tone they can relate to?

Founded in 1969, The National Military Family Association is dedicated to serving the families and survivors of the seven uniformed services through education, information, and advocacy. Most individuals in the military are between the ages of eighteen and thirty-seven, and the association largely serves their spouses, so its members and primary audiences for its programs are typically Generation Ys, or Millennials, as they're sometimes called.

Research into this generation's communications habits shows that they are extremely comfortable with newer communications channels such as e-mail, SMS (text) messaging, and social media tools like Twitter and Facebook. Association research into the communications preferences of military family members confirmed this too. In fact, military families are even more likely than other families to use online and mobile communications to receive news or communicate with others because they often relocate or are communicating with family members who may be deployed overseas.

Although most of the association's staff and board have family members who have served in the military, they tend to be a bit older than their target audience, and their communications preferences are a bit more reflective of older generations' habits. However, once they completed this research into the communications preferences of their members, their plans changed. It's now clearer where their limited outreach budget and staff resources should be allocated (online and in social media). This research also helped association board members understand the shift in the organization's communications.

The idea that your organization should communicate in the style that its target audience prefers is the basis of audience-centric communications.

Another terrific example of successful audience-centric communicating comes from the ASPCA, which began by asking a simple question: *Are dog people and cat people alike, or are cat people just interested in cats, and dog folks in dogs?* To answer this question, it created a test e-mail. The result of the test was unequivocal: cat people respond much more favorably when they receive content exclusively about cats, and vice versa. Today, if you register on the ASPCA Web site (www.aspca.org), you'll be asked to enter information about your pet(s). The types of communications you receive after that will be determined by this pet information. This change, one part of a new way of communicating that grew out of the ASPCA's strategic plan, helped this nonprofit virtually double its operating income in a few short years.

Does your organization . . .

- Communicate with audiences via each group's *preferred media* (in other words, people who like e-mail receive your e-mail, people who like calls get called, and so forth)?
- Use language that describes the *benefits* of its work to audiences in a way that they find meaningful and personally relevant?

- Adjust the *quantity* and *type of information* it sends to people based on their level of engagement with the organization?

Audience-centric communications are about communicating on the audience's terms, not our own.

Communicating with audience-centricity requires us to move from thinking from our own point of view toward thinking from other people's point of view. (If you're not sure where to begin, just ask them.)

Accessing Donor Feel-Good and the Warm Fuzzy

Individual donors give for a variety of reasons, such as these:

- They believe in the cause or vision of the organization.
- They were asked.
- They are motivated by emotions that include altruism, sympathy, pride, hope, fear, obligation, reciprocity, nostalgia, recognition, and a sense of community.
- They will receive tax credits or deductions.
- Giving is part of their faith or religion.
- They will be publicly acknowledged.
- Giving improves their social status or position.

But many organizations forget about these motivators when they write their year-end appeals, e-mail campaigns, or online donation pages. Instead, they emphasize a laundry list of programs—with little focus on the outcomes, benefits, or accomplishments.

The *feel-good* of giving may even be physically manifested. Research conducted at the University of Oregon (and subsequently published in *Science*) used brain imaging technology to map the effects giving had on test subjects. Although the results were mixed, about half of the test subjects' brain scans showed that they got a "warm glow" from giving, a feeling similar to what they'd experience from socializing with friends.

At the end of the day, most people will give because they are moved to do so: they have a feeling that it's the "right thing to do." So how do you create that feeling in a donor? A compelling story about an individual will yield much greater giving than the same story told from the point of view of how an entire community is affected. This is the *warm fuzzy*, the personal and emotional connection that people feel when a story moves them—and this happens most effectively at the one-to-one level.

Gaining Perspective

The more you know about something, the easier it can be to forget how little others know about it. The reasons why an organization is worth supporting are so clear to its staff that they may lose sight of the reality that outsiders aren't already believers. Once staff lose perspective on the difference between their connection to the organization and that of target audiences, they will often:

- Overdescribe the details of programs and services: that is, supply too much information.
- Forget to focus on the outcomes and benefits: in other words, the warm fuzzy content that explains why someone should care.

- Use jargon that's relevant to other professionals in this space but unfamiliar to clients or donors: for example, terms like *capacity-building* or *preventive services*.
- Forget to add a *call to action*: that is, a direct request for the reader to take action (typically, to make a gift, volunteer, or participate).
- Use language that's inappropriate for their audiences: for example, writing at a college-graduate reading level for programs that target those with less education or supplying more technical detail than donors want.

Implementing Audience-Centric Communications

Here are three ways you can begin shifting your organization towards a more audience-centric style of communicating:

- Conduct formal or informal research into your target audiences' preferred communications styles and channels. Use this research to shape the language you use, and the media through which you send messages.
- Develop a communications calendar built around the best times to reach your audiences (not around your organization's convenience, fiscal year, or other internal drivers).
- Implement software solutions, when possible, that allow you to specify the communications preferences of the individuals in your database so you can contact them in the way they prefer: for instance, e-mailing the people who prefer e-mail and have requested that you stop sending printed materials.

Doing More with Less

Regardless of their staff size, budget, or the surrounding economy, nonprofits rarely have the resources to communicate as much as they would like. Larger organizations with bigger budgets wish they could conduct high-visibility outreach campaigns, monitor the blogosphere and respond more proactively, or fully leverage social media. Organizations with less staff and smaller budgets wish they could build a better Web site or create a useful overview brochure. Although their communications objectives and needs may be different, all organizations grapple with one ongoing question: *How can we do more with less?*

Lack of Resources

Most nonprofits invested in Web sites several years ago and hoped would have a long shelf-life. By learning software programs like FrontPage and Dreamweaver, or even the coding language HTML, they hoped to maintain the site themselves so the content could stay current. Before 2006, very few people in the nonprofit sector saw Web 2.0 coming or considered the impact on their nonprofits of such new technologies as open-source software; low-cost; online digital video; and social media. Even today, many organizations are struggling to wrap their heads around YouTube, Flickr, social networking, and what these media mean to them. As a result, most organizations didn't budget for the Web upgrades they now find themselves making to stay current. In fact, changes in technology are so great and happening at such speed, it's likely that a nonprofit will need to build a new site or conduct major upgrades every two to three years.

When asked what the single biggest barrier to effective communications is in their organization, 27.8 percent of respondents to Big Duck's 2008 Barriers to Effective Communications survey cited not enough time, and 21.7 percent claimed lack of adequate budget.

Lack of Professional Communications Staff

The third most common barrier to effective communications is staff capacity. Often, the people who are in charge of communications at a nonprofit organization have little or no experience with nonprofit marketing or communications specifically. (Ideally, they would have not only nonprofit management expertise but also undergraduate or graduate degrees in communications.)

Organizations with larger operating budgets ($11 million or more annually) typically have dedicated communications staff (79 percent of those that completed Big Duck's Barriers survey), and their staff feel they have the ability to develop and manage communications effectively (54.6 percent). However, a majority of these organizations don't believe they have an adequate budget to cover communications activities (65.9 percent) and feel that producing outreach and fundraising materials is usually a stressful process (52.3 percent).

At smaller organizations (those with fewer than twenty-five people on the staff or annual operating budgets of less than $5 million), communications departments and staff people are less common (34.4 percent of these survey respondents have them), and their level of expertise is more likely to be in question.

Planning and budgeting for staff and not just for materials is important, even in smaller organizations, in order to move toward a long-view approach to communications. To survive downturns and recessions, you'll need staff people who are responsible for communicating proactively with your existing supporters and engaging new ones. With the rise of social media and online fundraising the costs of producing materials are dropping, but the time people must spend communicating online is growing.

Lack of Funding for Communications Changes

The cost of hiring professionals to help you refine communications will vary depending on how you structure the roles of staff, volunteers, freelancers, or agencies. Most often, organizations ask key supporters, often board members or long-term donors, to underwrite capacity-related changes in areas where staff have little or no skill (for instance, in design or Web development). Foundations may underwrite the creation of a development or communications position, for example, or a board member with marketing experience may fund work on messaging. Making a compelling case for this type of support can be challenging when it comes to organization leaders or donors out of the blue. A long-view approach will help you integrate these *asks* into plans and budgets when most appropriate. So don't wait until you desperately need that new identity, Web site, or printed material and then try to figure out how to pay for it. Instead, connect the ideas and information you need to communicate with larger organizational objectives (often derived from strategic planning) and explain that connection to organizational leaders during budgeting periods. This approach also holds true for funding professional development among communications staff.

In addition, here are a few suggestions to help you do more with less:

- Before the fiscal year begins, plan and budget for communications activities, and make sure you carve out a defined budget.
- Assign someone—staff or volunteer—to manage and be responsible for implementing the communications budget and calendar. In addition to making it happen, they should be responsible for tracking the results of each piece. This person should report back regularly, at staff, management, or board meetings, to ensure accountability and assess the return on investment.
- Monitor the nonprofit landscape to see how your peers are communicating regularly. Look for them in social media (do they have a Facebook presence or YouTube video, for instance?), visit their Web sites, and sign up to receive their publications. Report back to your organization's leaders on their work and the buzz you hear about it. You might also ask staff or consultants to present case studies from other organizations. Use these presentations to facilitate a discussion about your own organization's communications strengths and challenges.

In Summary

- Seeing the long view, managing information saturation, communicating on your audiences' terms, and doing more with less are basic principles that help organizations communicate effectively.

- Seeing the long view requires maintaining perspective on the bigger picture and using it to inform decisions, even while you manage day-to-day communications.

- Getting attention is harder than ever. With more ways to communicate and more and more organizations using them, it's important to have a strategy that will help you leverage your investment in communications as fully as possible.

- Most organizations communicate on their own terms—not their audiences'. Shifting toward an audience-centric point of view can be transformative.

- Institutional challenges such as politics, limited staff or expertise, small or nonexistent budgets, and a tendency to work reactively often lead to accidental brands, and last-minute materials. These communications are usually far from optimal and get redone over time, using up additional resources.

- In an ideal world, nonprofits would budget and staff appropriately for communications from the beginning. Because most can't do this, shifting the culture toward a long view will take time and effort. Budgets, dedicated staff, and calendars can help.

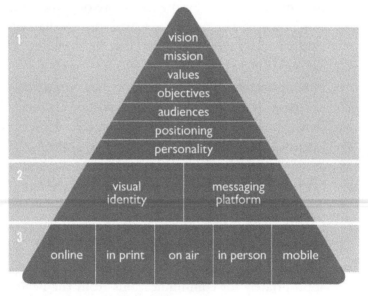

1. **ORGANIZATIONAL LEVEL:** Includes the core elements that direct all aspects of the organization's work

2. **IDENTITY LEVEL:** What most people think of as *branding*—specifically, the visual identity and messaging platform

3. **EXPERIENTIAL LEVEL:** The channels and tools through which audiences connect with the organization

CHAPTER 3

Overview of Brandraising

Establishing *vision, mission, values, objectives, audiences, positioning*, and *personality* before creative work occurs ensures that all communications are reflective of an organization's true reason for existence. This chapter outlines the basic structure of brandraising and introduces the concepts covered in more depth in the chapters that follow. The brandraising graphic on the facing page shows how all aspects of communications fit together into a cohesive structure. The left-hand side of this *information visualization* briefly describes the three levels of brandraising: Organizational, Identity, and Experiential.

The Organizational Level

The top seven elements of the brandraising structure make up the Organizational Level because they directly drive programs, the human resource (HR) function, and most organizational decisions, not just communications. These elements are

- *Vision*: the notion of a better world that might be achieved and the idea that originally sparked the creation of the organization (the *why*)
- *Mission*: the expression of what this organization will do (*how* the *why* of the vision will be achieved)
- *Values*: the organization's belief system, which guides its approach
- *Objectives*: the specific goals that must be achieved for the organization to fulfill its mission
- *Audiences*: the varied groups of constituents the organization must reach and inspire to action in order to achieve its objectives
- *Positioning*: the essence of how the organization is different from others in the same space (such as peer organizations)
- *Personality*: the tone and style, or attitude, of all communications

Positioning and personality may be the least familiar of these terms for most nonprofit professionals. Although they're tried-and-true marketing concepts used widely in the corporate sector, they are rarely applied in the social sector. Chapter Four, "Brandraising at the Organizational Level," will cover all these elements in greater detail.

The Identity Level

The Identity Level includes the pieces most people think of when they hear the word *brand*.

- The *visual identity platform* includes the logos, colors, typefaces, and images used to communicate.
- The *messaging platform* includes *written* messages such as the organization's name and tagline; vision, mission, and values statements; key messages; and other predefined, inflexible elements that should be used consistently. It also includes the *elevator pitch*, a short (often memorized) spoken statement used to briefly introduce the organization.

Chapter Five will discuss this level in detail.

The Experiential Level

The Experiential Level defines the ways audiences interact with the organization. It includes

- *Online* channels, such as the organization's Web site, e-mail, blogs, and social media presence.
- *In print* communications, such as brochures, magazine or news articles, flyers, and reports.
- *In person* spaces where programs, meetings, galas, or other gatherings are held.
- *On air* communications, such as public service announcements (PSAs) or other ads on TV or radio, videos on YouTube, and coverage by journalists in these media.
- *Mobile* communications that reach people by cell phone, often by text messaging—a powerful newer channel that many organizations are now using for advocacy and fundraising.

Chapter Six will focus on this level.

Leadership Involvement in Each Level

Organizational Level elements are usually founder-driven in a nonprofit's early years and shaped by the board in later years. Executive leaders (typically the board and senior staff) should participate in developing these elements and in approving any changes to them downstream. Many leaders move quickly through discussions about what the organization's future should be like, what the organization exists to do, or what deeply held beliefs frame its work, with the result that these leaders (and their staff) then dive into details before they have clearly expressed the organization's vision, mission, values, and objectives. However, these elements provide the strategic underpinning of the organization and are as essential for programs as they are for good communications.

Identity Level elements should remain consistent throughout all communications; therefore, they should change infrequently. They should be subject to regular oversight from a staff person (ideally, one with communications experience). In very small organizations (those with operating budgets of less than $1 million, for example), the Identity Level is typically overseen and managed by the executive director. In small to midsize organizations (with budgets ranging from approximately $1 million to $5 million), oversight may be provided by a development director whose job description includes managing communications. In larger organizations, a communications or external affairs director is likely to oversee work at the Identity Level.

In many organizations, staff people will typically enforce the Identity Level on a daily basis to ensure consistency, and the executive director (or other chief officer) will direct any needed development of or changes to Identity Level elements, with the board's approval and participation in the process. In addition to voting on whether or not to approve new logos or messaging, board members should play a role in Identity Level brandraising by sharing their points of view and using the Identity elements that have been created consistently.

For example, developing or changing the mission statement requires the executive director's active participation and approval and then, at a minimum, a board-level vote to adopt any new language. Then the director of communications (or, in smaller organizations, the executive director or director of development) will typically be responsible for ensuring that the approved mission statement is used, exactly as written, on all materials at the Experiential Level.

The Experiential Level is managed by the staff who are responsible for communications. In smaller organizations they are program staff who are responsible for promoting their own events and projects. In bigger organizations, development or communications departments will produce materials in-house or with help from volunteers, freelancers, or agencies.

Measuring and Assessing Brandraising's Impact

Brandraising will take time, money, and effort. It's a long-view strategy. Is it worth it for your organization?

Clear, consistent communications distinguish your organization from others who are competing for the same donors, funders, participants, and media attention. In good times, that's nice even though perhaps not essential. In bad times, it becomes critical for survival.

In addition, nonprofit staff will reap important benefits from developing clearer communications in a more cohesive system. When new materials (at the Experiential Level) need to be developed, staff with clearly defined Organizational and Identity Level elements can work faster and with a greater likelihood that the end result will be consistent and powerful, because they don't have to start from scratch. Staff will also be better equipped to work independently and stay on track because the guidelines for success and the elements they can work with are predefined.

Brandraising can also attract and retain better staff for the organization by expressing its strengths clearly and effectively, whereas subpar communications (for instance, a poor Web site) will mask the organization's abilities and impact.

Once a brandraising system exists in your organization, your donors, prospects, clients, and other audiences will hear, read, and see the same messages at each point of contact they have with your organization. Therefore,

- The impressions they will form are more likely to be true to what your organization wants to convey, because you are in the driver's seat directing those impressions.
- The image of your organization will be consistent across all media, which sends a signal that the organization is "buttoned up." This consistency leads

audiences to infer credibility, reassurance, and reliability.

- Your audiences are more likely to pay attention to your organization's communications because they recognize them and feel they provide useful content that's relevant to them.
- During hard economic times, your organization is more likely to stand out from the pack and look like a solid investment.

Brandraising will also help to ensure that your board members can be counted on to describe the organization accurately and consistently, rather than exclusively from their own point of view. When individuals become confident they are *on message*, they are more likely to talk about and promote the organization. As a result they'll introduce new relationships, such as potential new board members or donors. Moreover, actually recruiting these people and other desirable board members and donors becomes easier when your organization presents itself clearly.

But here's the rub: you can't develop a strong brandraising structure overnight. Like barn raising, it takes planning, coordination, and teamwork. Brandraising is a long-view strategy that takes months to develop and requires ongoing maintenance to be fully beneficial.

Quantitative and Qualitative Metrics

The impact of brandraising can be measured *quantitatively* and *qualitatively*. Quantitative metrics are useful because they are measurable, reflecting such facts as the number of individuals who graduate from a program and are successfully employed three years later, the number of dollars raised, the percentage of respondents who gave to an appeal, and so forth.

Qualitative measurements are also valuable even though less specific. Anecdotal feedback from a key donor about your newsletter, new visual identity, or other communications might be extremely valuable, but it can be difficult to say whether this person's point of view represents that of others too. Often, staff are the ones who capture and relay the most valuable qualitative feedback, because they hear what people say as they interact with your organization.

When organizations strive to change perception about an issue, or even to change behavior, they are engaging in *social marketing*. Effective social marketing campaigns have resulted in increased social acceptance of condom use, greater compliance in wearing helmets and seat belts, and have led to a decline in the acceptability of drinking and driving, for instance. These shifts can be measured quantitatively by conducting opinion research polls (typically done by market research companies over the telephone). By repeating the same survey at periodic intervals (every six months or annually) and comparing results, researchers can begin to identify trends.

For some organizations, the impact of brandraising is immediately evident and measurable. Staff people become more efficient and effective communicators, allowing them to focus more on other aspects of their work. Board members feel more comfortable fundraising on the agency's behalf because they now have the better tools for doing it.

In Summary

- Chapter Three provides a high-level overview of the three levels of brandraising: the Organizational Level, the Identity Level, and the Experiential Level. The chapters that follow outline the elements of each level in greater detail.
- Seeing communications as an integrated whole, rather than as a series of tactical tools, will ensure consistency and cohesion.
- Brandraising is a long-view strategy that pays off over time by ensuring that the contents and presentation of organizational communications are consistent and driven by the organization's vision and mission.
- Because brandraising is a long-view strategy, it requires planning, coordination, and collaboration; it's valuable to make sure everyone, and particularly every leader, understands his or her role in the process.
- The value of brandraising can be measured qualitatively and quantitatively over time.

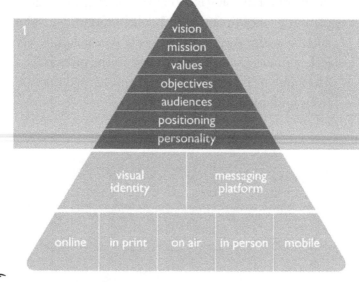

vision
mission
values
objectives
audiences
positioning
personality

visual identity | messaging platform

online | in print | on air | in person | mobile

1. ORGANIZATIONAL LEVEL: Includes the core elements that direct all aspects of the organization's work

CHAPTER 4

Brandraising at the Organizational Level

Vision, *mission*, *values*, *objectives*, and *audiences* drive all aspects of an organization's work—including programs, fundraising, and advocacy at all levels—whether they are formally defined or not. The task of formally defining these elements is typically carried out at the board level, with significant participation from staff leaders and perhaps with the help of organizational development consultants as well. The Organizational Level elements of *positioning* and *personality* are usually less familiar to people with limited experience in marketing or communications, but they can be equally vital to a nonprofit's work.

This chapter will explore how the elements of the Organizational Level affect the ways nonprofits communicate, and how these elements form the strategic platform for the Identity and Experiential Levels.

What Comes First: Strategic Planning or Brandraising?

In high-functioning nonprofits a clear vision and mission, defined and supported by organizational leaders, are the most important of the elements that drive all aspects of the work. Without clarity on what the organization exists to do and how it will do it, it's difficult to communicate clearly and consistently. With little strategy driving them, communications activities and other functions will devolve into a series of tactical, day-to-day activities, leading to poor results. In established organizations, for instance, those that have been around for more than five years, brandraising efforts often follow strategic planning. If your organization is considering going through a strategic planning process soon, hold off undertaking a major shift in your communications until that work is complete.

Before brandraising begins, the organization's staff and board should be on the same page about where the nonprofit is heading for the long term. In addition to greatly improving communications with all stakeholders, this shared clarity and purpose, articulated through the elements covered in this chapter, can improve creative work by minimizing subjective reactions ("I don't like that logo") and keeping the team oriented along more strategic lines ("that logo doesn't work because it doesn't reflect our values [or doesn't encompass one of our objectives]").

Vision

In 1994, residents of a rural community in central Massachusetts noticed that developers were buying up more and more farmland. Fields that had once been filled with crops were increasingly being transformed into neighborhoods with prefab houses as it became more profitable for farmers to sell their land to developers than to farm it. Their rural, bucolic community was changing and becoming more suburban. A group of concerned people got together and started asking questions. How much development is good for a community, and how much is too much? How can we retain the rural nature of our area without it becoming too expensive or rarified? How can we save the farmlands that have been the backbone of our community and make it profitable to farm? As a result, the East Quabbin Land Trust was formed. By the end of 2008, these volunteers (they hired their first paid staff person recently) had protected over 2,500 acres.

Most organizations begin because an individual or a group identifies a problem and wants to work toward a solution. Often, their vision of how things should be is so large that achieving it is beyond what any single organization could do alone; it will take the combined efforts of many over time.

Visions are big ideas. *Vision statements* are the big ideas written down in a way that can be shared. Although all organizations emerge out of some sort of vision, many do not formally define that vision in a written statement. (Instead, they focus on mission.) In his book *Guiding Growth: How Vision Keeps Companies on Course* (2003), author Mark Lipton argues that it is clarity of vision more than any specific strategy that keeps both nonprofits and for-profits on course, particularly during periods of growth.

As years go by, organizations may expand, evolve, or take on a new point of view. Visions may become less clear as the founder departs and other changes in leadership or the external environment occur. Typically, the vision is revisited and explored during strategic planning or other organizational development work involving the board. Fundamentally, revisiting the vision is to ask, What should the future look like?

Mission

If a nonprofit's vision of changing the world could be described as a pie, then its mission would be the slice of work the organization has carved out specifically for itself. Other slices of the pie might be addressed by other organizations with some shared vision but a different focus. Missions are therefore more specific and descriptive of the actual work to be undertaken by a nonprofit—not just the good it hopes to achieve in broad terms.

In 2003, BoardSource (www.boardsource.org) published *The Nonprofit Board's Role in Setting and Advancing the Mission,* by Kay Sprinkel Grace, as part of its Governance Series. This booklet outlines ways a nonprofit board may develop its mission, shares examples of effective *mission statements,* and provides a solid process for developing a mission. Specifically, Grace advises that any exploration of mission begin with the questions, *Why do we exist?* and, *What will we do?* She encourages boards to focus on concepts and ideas before they get caught up in the semantics of crafting a powerful mission statement. In addition to formulating the mission, a nonprofit board's primary responsibility is to ensure that the organization is fulfilling its mission and staying on track.

A strong mission answers the basic question of what the organization exists to do and provides a basis for judging the success of the organization and its key programs. That is why your organization's mission must drive communications and all other organizational activities. Do your communications, including your newsletter, e-mail, and new social network, clearly relate back to your mission? The objective of each communication and its relationship to your organization's mission should be clear.

Pat Furlong, a nurse whose two sons had been diagnosed with Duchenne muscular dystrophy, founded Parent Project Muscular Dystrophy in 1994. Duchenne is a terminal, genetic disorder that primarily affects boys. If untreated, boys with Duchenne typically die in their teens. When Pat began researching treatments and standards of care, she found that few existed. Almost immediately, she connected with other parents of sons with Duchenne and founded the organization with this vision: "to create a world in which boys with Duchenne can survive and thrive into adulthood and beyond."

This vision is large and transformative, and Parent Project Muscular Dystrophy can't do it alone. To achieve it, this organization must collaborate with researchers, scientists, policymakers, families, and others. Its mission statement—"to improve the treatment, quality of life and long-term outlook for all individuals affected by Duchenne muscular dystrophy (Duchenne) through research, advocacy, education, and compassion" (www .parentprojectmd.org)—is also ambitious, but much more specific about the work it will focus on. This statement defines a slice of the vision that emphasizes a four-pronged strategy (research, advocacy, education, and compassion), and a focus on Duchenne.

Revising the Mission

Revising an organization's mission is typically an outgrowth of strategic planning or other organizational development work. In some organizations the board formally reviews the mission every one to five years, either at a retreat or in a facilitated discussion during a board meeting. Too often, however, mission discussions focus on the language of the mission statement before the board has fully explored whether the piece of pie the mission has carved out—the idea itself—is still relevant.

Missions usually change when the core work the organization set out to do has been completed or when the environment has changed enough to warrant a serious rethinking of purpose. For example, the March of Dimes was founded in 1938 with the mission of curing polio. After the polio vaccine was declared effective, in 1958, the March of Dimes shifted its mission toward saving babies from birth defects.

Crafting the Mission Statement

Missions are expressed through written mission statements. Most mission statements are carefully crafted, board-approved, and used exactly as originally written, or *verbatim*, in all communications.

In some organizations, staff will find themselves tinkering with the language of their mission statement in order to suit a particular audience, grant application, or other need. These sorts of alterations usually indicate that the mission statement is no longer adequately articulating the organization's work, and they can lead to *mission creep*, taking on work that's not directly relevant (often because funding is available). Instead of making edits along the way, it's better for staff and board leadership to revisit the *idea* of the mission, then consider the language that will express the current idea, and thus arrive at a newer version of the mission statement that works universally.

When well-chosen, the language of the mission statement will express the mission dynamically, using the *personality* of the organization and communicating the organization's *positioning* (core concepts covered later in this chapter). It should be so effective that tinkering with it will be unnecessary.

Some staff and board people will approach the process of writing a new mission statement with preconceived ideas about how long it should be. Often, there's a perception that a mission statement should be very short—perhaps only one sentence long, for instance. There's no right or wrong length for a mission statement. In fact, there are no hard or fast rules in mission statement construction that apply universally to all organizations. What's important is that the statement expresses the concept of the organization's mission—what it exists to do—clearly and effectively. If you can do that effectively in one sentence, that's terrific. For some organizations, however, it's not realistic to be that brief.

Exhibit 4.1 contains actual examples of nonprofit mission statements that show a range of approaches. They vary in length, complexity, use of jargon, and structure. Each communicates uniquely about the organization's personality.

EXHIBIT 4.1 Examples of Nonprofit Mission Statements

Slow Food USA

Slow Food USA envisions a future food system that is based on the principles of high quality and taste, environmental sustainability, and social justice—in essence, a food system that is good, clean and fair. We seek to catalyze a broad cultural shift away from the destructive effects of an industrial food system and fast life; toward the regenerative cultural, social and economic benefits of a sustainable food system, regional food traditions, the pleasures of the table, and a slower and more harmonious rhythm of life [www.slowfoodusa.org].

Brooklyn Botanic Garden

The mission of Brooklyn Botanic Garden is to serve all the people in its community and throughout the world by:

- Displaying plants and practicing the high art of horticulture to provide a beautiful and hospitable setting for the delight and inspiration of the public.
- Engaging in research in plant sciences to expand human knowledge of plants, and disseminating the results to science professionals and the general public.
- Teaching children and adults about plants at a popular level, as well as making available instruction in the exacting skills required to grow plants and make beautiful gardens.
- Reaching out to help the people of all our diverse urban neighborhoods to enhance the quality of their surroundings and their daily lives through the cultivation and enjoyment of plants.
- Seeking actively to arouse public awareness of the fragility of our natural environment, both local and global, and providing information about ways to conserve and protect it [www.bbg.org].

Betty Ford Center

To provide effective alcohol and other drug dependency treatment services, including programs of education and research to help women, men and families begin the process of recovery [www.BettyFordCenter.org].

Because it's used externally, not just internally, an effective mission statement uses *audience-centric* language: that is, language designed to communicate with a particular audience in their own terms in order to help people understand what the organization is and does. These questions can help you assess how effective your organization's mission statement is:

- Does our mission statement clearly express what it is we do?
- Does it use language that our audiences understand and relate to?
- Does it inspire our audiences to want to get involved, take action, or connect with us?
- Is it reflective of our values, positioning, and personality?

Values

Values are beliefs in which a person or group has an emotional investment. In an organization, values can serve as guiding principles that shape and inform the organization's approach to its work.

The Opportunity Agenda is a project of the Tides Foundation, which was founded to expand opportunity in America. This project works with communications and the media to build public support, work with nonprofits, conduct research, and work on related policy issues. Exhibit 4.2 lists its "core values," which drive all aspects of its work and are published on its Web site.

EXHIBIT 4.2 Opportunity Agenda's Values

We believe that true opportunity requires a commitment to a core set of values. These values are integrally related to the principle of human rights. Equal treatment, a voice in societal decisions, a chance to start over, and the tools to meet our own basic needs are not just good policy ideas. They are the right of every human being simply by virtue of his or her humanity.

Mobility—Where we start out in life should not determine where we end up. Inherent in mobility is the belief that everyone who works hard should be able to advance and participate fully in society. Mobility requires that our nation's class distinctions be fluid and unpredictable over generations, while moving forward as a society.

Equality—The benefits and burdens of society should not depend on what we look like or where we come from. Equality requires that we celebrate our differences while challenging stereotypes and breaking down barriers. Equality is both the absence of discrimination and the presence of fairness.

Voice—We should all have a say in the decisions that affect us. Our voices must be heard in voting booths, at public forums and across the media. Expanding opportunity requires that we listen to the ideas, hopes, and dreams of everyone who lives here.

Redemption—We all grow and change over time and need a chance to start over when things go wrong. To foster redemption, we must provide conditions that allow people to develop, to rebuild, and to reclaim full responsibility for their lives.

Community—We share responsibility for each other, and the strength of our nation depends on the vibrancy and cohesiveness of our diverse population. With a strong sense of community, we understand that opportunity is not only about personal success but about our success as a people.

Security—We should all have the tools to meet our own basic needs and the needs of our families. Without economic and social security, it is impossible to access the other rights and responsibilities society has to offer. Security is at the core of our human dignity [www .opportunityagenda.org].

At an organization that considers equality or inclusion a key value, it would be logical to include all staff in discussions before key decisions were made that might affect them. Similarly, an organization that considered environmental sustainability a core value would be unlikely to partner with a business that demonstrated a poor track record of environmental stewardship (for instance, a manufacturer of huge SUVs). It might also place a high value on printing with soy-based ink on recycled paper.

These examples demonstrate how values are brought to life through daily activities and decision making; they are not just abstract concepts. How strictly an organization adheres to its values during the day-to-day is often a function of its culture, and how the executive director or other leadership model their importance through their own management styles.

Values are typically defined by leaders of both the staff and the board and then approved by the board. The process typically begins with a conversation about the deeply held beliefs that shape the organization's work. To start this process at your nonprofit, convene a meeting with the appropriate board and staff members (the number involved will depend on the size and structure of your organization). Working as a group, develop a list of values that influence how work is done at the organization. Pare the list down by asking, "Which values are essential to what we do and how we do it?" It can also be helpful to discuss which values differentiate your organization from peer organizations. Lastly, identify and discuss the values that individuals feel so strongly about that they would consider leaving the organization if these values were no longer important. Later on, the values selected by this group and approved by the board can be expressed in a *values statement*, which is part of your *messaging platform* (as discussed in Chapter Five).

Organizational values rarely change. When they do, the change often takes place over many years, as vision and mission changes coupled with staff turnover lead to shifts in culture. Reviewing and discussing values whenever vision and mission are discussed can ensure that your nonprofit's values remain relevant and can help staff remember to apply these values every day to guide management and decision making.

Objectives

Strategic planning processes often result in a plan that defines a set of objectives that the organization will work toward to achieve its mission. If all the objectives are fulfilled, then the mission will be achieved. Organizational objectives are extremely useful for setting forth a framework for annual budgeting and planning, and like the other elements of the Organizational Level, they affect all aspects of an organization's work—not just its communications. This framework can help your organization answer questions such as these:

- What resources and activities should be assigned to each objective in the next fiscal year?
- If we have a budget deficit, which objectives can we shift resources away from?
- If a new project is developed or new idea emerges, which objectives does it advance? Does it relate to objectives that are priorities for us?

EXHIBIT 4.3 Parent Project Muscular Dystrophy's
Objectives

- To identify, support, and share promising Duchenne-related research.
- To make state-of-the-art information about treatment and care options available to all members of the Duchenne community.
- To pursue strategies that will impact this generation of young men affected by Duchenne as well as future generations.
- To encourage policymakers to afford the same priority to Duchenne as they would to other disorders of similar incidence and prevalence.
- To create a supportive community for people affected by Duchenne.
- To participate actively in the international Duchenne community.
- To ensure that Duchenne is managed, developed, and funded in a manner consistent with nonprofit industry best practices [www .parentprojectmd.org].

Exhibit 4.3 displays Parent Project Muscular Dystrophy's objectives.

The organization's staff use these objectives to set operational plans in advance of each fiscal year and to budget accordingly to accomplish the plans. The board of directors then reviews and approves the budget. In addition, as new ideas or projects are suggested during the year, staff can use these objectives in determining whether an idea or project should be integrated into the organization's work and what resources can be allocated to it.

How Objectives Inform Communications

Objectives make it easier to assess priorities and identify mission creep. Therefore they help staff determine which communications are most connected to advancing the mission. For example, for many years, Parent Project Muscular Dystrophy prioritized its objective of creating "a supportive community for people affected by Duchenne." This objective led to the creation of a social networking site (http://community.parentprojectmd.org) where members of the Parent Project Muscular Dystrophy community can chat in various forums, post pictures and videos, ask questions, and help each other. The organization's president actively blogs and engages in dialogue with members of the community, too.

Defining Objectives

A nonprofit organization's vision, mission, values, and objectives are all typically defined by its leaders, often with the help of consultants or external advisers and typically through a strategic-planning process. During this process, the defining of objectives *unpacks* the specific goals that must be reached in order to achieve the mission, making it more tangible. Once objectives are clearly defined, they can be used to plan and budget effectively before a new fiscal year. Just as important, they can be used to constantly assess progress throughout the year and to inform decisions about what the organization will or won't do as new challenges and opportunities emerge.

Refining Objectives

Although objectives are most scrutinized during periods of change or planning (such as the start of a new fiscal year), they shouldn't sit on the shelf the rest of the time. Instead, leaders can use them as a framework for reporting on progress at board and staff meetings and for benchmarking the work of key departments.

Over the course of time it often becomes clear that some objectives are more vital and active than others. They come up over and over again and typically receive the greatest allocations of staff and budget. As plans are being made for the upcoming fiscal year in your organization, a discussion about the vitality and relevance of each objective may not only inform your budgeting process but also suggest that it's time to take a closer look at your objectives overall.

Audiences

Most organizations have an intuitive sense of the individuals and groups that make up their audiences. Audiences fall into three categories:

- *Fundraising audiences*, consisting of individuals, corporations, foundations, or the government (or a combination of these)
- *Program audiences*, consisting of clients, individuals, or organizations who receive services; patrons; or members (or a combination of these)
- *Advocacy audiences*, consisting of community leaders, policymakers, the media, or key issue influencers (or a combination of these)

Connecting Audiences and Objectives

Rarely do organizations formally articulate who their audiences are and then deliberately link them to specific objectives. But doing so doesn't take long, and it yields real clarity that helps organizations avoid wasting time and money later in their communications at the Identity and Experiential Levels.

For example, in order to achieve its objectives (and therefore its mission), Parent Project Muscular Dystrophy must communicate effectively with

- Individuals and families affected by Duchenne
- Scientists and other professionals whose work focuses on Duchenne
- Policymakers and their staff
- Other organizations that focus on Duchenne (peers)
- Funders of all kinds
- Media that report on health and science issues

These audiences represent diverse interests in Duchenne muscular dystrophy. If you listed the groups and individuals your organization must communicate with in order to be successful, who would they be?

Most nonprofits have diverse target audiences, often with little or no overlap. Their clients can be totally different from their donors, for instance. This diversity of audiences makes communicating inherently more complex. (In fact, I believe it is the primary reason why creating communications for nonprofits is more challenging than creating them for for-profits; in for-profits most activities are focused on reaching just one audience—the customer.)

Using Audience Personas

Nonprofit staff tend to use impersonal labels like *donor, member, client,* or *blogger* when talking about audiences.

But these classifications can be too broad and reflect only the organization's needs. Sure, you need donors to support your nonprofit and clients to work with, but what do they want from you? What's in it for them? It's easy to forget that there are living, breathing individuals out there and that people who may share a common label (for instance, *donors*) can be extremely different from one another in the reasons why they care about your organization and in the results or benefits they're looking for from you.

Creating *audience personas* can help you get beyond broad labels and think about your constituents in more audience-centric terms. (Audience-centrism is also discussed in Chapters Two and Six.) Start with your donors. What types of people typically support your organization? Do they fall into subcategories that might help you understand them better? For instance, could you speculate that members of one donor group are likely to be community residents, middle class, concerned about a particular issue, and comfortable giving less than $100 each year? If so, put a name and a face to that type of person. What you're doing is defining an individual who represents a group of people. You might use a real donor in your database, or just grab a photo online and give the person in it a fictitious name. Below the image, write down some ideas you have about who this representative donor might be and what motivates her to care about or engage with your organization. Is she single? Does she have kids? What does she do for a living? What does she do for fun? Why does she support your organization? How often and through what channels is she likely to want to hear from you?

For example, a community center might create a persona for a fictional community resident named Mary. She's married, has two teenage kids, and works full time, as does her husband. She's constantly on the move and uses a BlackBerry to stay connected and organized. She and her husband are interested in making their community safer and participating in local activities. This persona is loosely based on the staff's experience with program participants and donors—not on one specific individual.

With what we know about Mary (and people like her), it might be safe to assume that reaching her digitally (for instance, via e-mail or a text messaging) might be more effective than phoning her. It might also be fair to assume that she'd prefer shorter, focused communications, rather than longer communications (such as a twelve-page newsletter) that require a lot of time to read.

Audience personas help turn an abstract group like *donors* into real people, with motivations, frustrations, and expectations. It can be helpful to create five to ten different personas, loosely representing the types of audiences you want to reach. Although this limited number won't fully represent the point of view of everyone in your fundraising, programs or advocacy universe, they'll come in handy as you brandraise. As you create new communications, use your audience personas on an ongoing basis by putting yourself in their shoes and asking, What would this person want to find on our Web site? How would he or she find us? Would he or she find this newsletter interesting? You might even tape the persona descriptions up on the wall for easy reference. By asking these questions and placing yourself in audiences' shoes, you're likely to make smarter decisions about how you communicate with each audience group.

Organizations can base their audience personas on formal or informal research they've conducted through interviewing, surveying, and screening. The obvious benefit of using real data is that they will add authenticity.

It's also beneficial to ask audiences for feedback on communications. Most major donors, for example, are regularly asked for gifts face to face. But how often do they get a call from the executive director or development director asking their opinion about something (maybe the new e-newsletter, for instance) after the gift has been made? Some organizations go as far as sharing logos, key messages, Web site designs, and other brandraising elements in progress to see how the individuals they are designed to appeal to will react to them.

Positioning

In 1980, two of the marketing world's most respected thinkers published *Positioning: The Battle for Your Mind*. In this book Al Ries and Jack Trout describe a position as the *single idea we hope to own in the minds of our target audiences*. Inherent in positioning is the goal of differentiating: making sure that what your audiences think about you is *different* from what they think of your peers. Although positioning is an unfamiliar concept to most people in the nonprofit sector, it can be extremely useful for bridging the gap between Organizational Level elements such as vision and mission and day-to-day fundraising communications.

When asked what they think of when they hear the name Red Cross, most people will answer "disaster relief." If you ask people what they associate with the March of Dimes, most will answer "fighting birth defects." Both of these are examples of clear positions that organizations have established in people's minds over decades of consistent communications. In the for-profit world, positioning is sometimes referred to as a USP, or *unique selling proposition*—a marketing term that grew out of the advertising industry. A USP is that special something that makes one product different from others. Johnson & Johnson's "no more tears" positioning, asserting that unlike the competition's baby shampoo, theirs won't sting your baby's eyes, has ensured for decades that their product leads the baby shampoo market. Similarly, Ivory soap asserted its leadership for generations with its "99.9% pure" claim. After all, who doesn't want pure soap?

Positioning defines what makes your organization unique, and what the *big idea* is that you hope to establish in the minds of your audiences. Here, for example, is the National Brain Tumor Society's *positioning statement*: "National Brain Tumor Society is the leading organization in the United States that funds critical research and offers comprehensive services to those affected by brain tumors." And this is the National Military Family Association's positioning statement: "National Military Family Association is *the* voice for military families—advocating on their behalf and responding to meet their needs."

Using Positioning

Once finalized, positioning serves as a strategic yardstick that all Identity and Experiential Level communications can be measured against. If an organization is changing its visual identity, its positioning should be shared with the design team in a brief defining what a new logo and supporting elements should communicate. Once logo options are presented, they can be assessed against the positioning, rather than just subjectively. The question on the table can be, "Which of these designs most accurately reflects our positioning?" Focusing the discussion around this question helps participants move away from the natural tendency to make subjective comments ("that reminds me of a carpet I had as a child," or, "I never liked brown") toward a more productive shared point of view.

This question also helps organizations assess their work strategically at the Experiential Level: for instance, when reviewing copy for a new brochure, newsletter design, public service announcement (PSA), or virtually any other element in the brandraising structure.

How Positioning Is Different from Mission

Positioning language typically isn't used publicly, because it often includes bold or even arrogant claims, such as "leader" or "only," that would likely irritate peers, program partners, and other key constituents. However, this assertive quality also serves to spark the passions of staff and board members by inspiring them to aim for the top. Positioning is like planting a flag on top of a mountain and claiming it as your organization's turf. Because that claim may be viewed as competitive or arrogant, it's often used internally. In contrast, mission statements are written to be shared. Although mission statements and positioning statements may express similar concepts, mission statements often describe the organization's work in more depth and complexity.

Defining Positioning

Positioning should grow out of a clear mission (and the vision that inspired it). If the nonprofit is in a period of reinvention where the mission is in flux, it's probably not the best time to try to establish clear positioning (see page 42 for more on the relationship of brandraising and strategic planning).

Defining positioning can be very hard to do in-house. Staff and board members are close to the nonprofit's work and its nuances, so they usually find it difficult to boil that work down to its bare essence. A consultant will arrive at positioning through a careful audit of your organization's materials, a review of your peers and competitors, discussions with leaders, and perhaps additional research. If working with a consultant proves unrealistic, it's best to approach positioning as an iterative process, with preliminary ideas solicited from board members and staff either via discussion or in writing. Using these ideas as a basis, an individual (typically the director of communications, director of development, or executive director) or a small working group generates a positioning draft, and subsequent refinements are made through discussions at the leadership level.

Personality

For years, Apple Computer ran an ad campaign that featured two men talking with each other. One was a casual-looking guy with shaggy hair and jeans who identified himself by saying, "Hi. I'm a Mac." He was standing next to a frumpy-looking guy wearing a bad suit and nerdy glasses who said, "And I'm a PC." These two embodied the disparate personalities that Apple Computer wanted viewers to associate with it and with its competitor: chiefly, that Macs are *casual, relaxed, hip,* and *functional,* and PCs are *out of touch, uptight, tired,* and *not at all cutting-edge.* This ad campaign is a great example of organizational personality expressed creatively in the for-profit world.

An organization's personality can be defined with a list of attributes that reflect the way the organization wants individuals to experience it. Imagine two different organizations, both with missions focusing on greenhouse gas reductions. The personality one of them hopes to achieve may be *measured, credible, comprehensive, reliable,* and *professional,* whereas the other nonprofit, with similar programs, might hope to be described as *responsive, agile, innovative, insightful,* and *grassroots.* Both personalities reflect positive qualities, but they are inherently different.

Using Personality

The adjectives that define a nonprofit's personality should be used to inspire the work that happens at the Identity Level in its brandraising structure. Continuing the example of the two organizations with similar missions but different personalities, we can expect the first organization to use an understated logo design, a muted color palette, a high-concept tagline, and written language that tends to feel conservative or formal. The second organization would likely use contemporary design elements, fonts, and colors (for instance, orange or lime green). It would tend to use language that's informal and reflective of current trends. It might even have controversial names for its programs or use imagery, ideas, and language that generates buzz. (Chapter Seven describes more of the day-to-day practicalities of using personality in communications.)

Defining Personality

The right personality is reflective of both what your organization really is and how you'd like audiences to perceive it. If it's too lofty or pie-in-the-sky, it will ring false and feel disconnected from your work. At the same time, your nonprofit should put its best foot forward, expressing its strengths, not its weaknesses.

You can begin the process of defining your organization's personality by arranging a series of interviews, phone calls, or group meetings with the organization's key constituents. The full board and, if not the entire staff, at least the senior-level staff should participate in this exercise. Ask these participants to visualize the organization they'd like to see in the future. (It may be a somewhat idealized version of the organization.)

Then ask them the following questions:

1. If this future organization had a theme song or anthem, what would it be? Why?
2. If this organization had a mascot or "power animal," what would it be? Why?
3. If this organization were a car, what type and color would it be? Why?

These questions will elicit smiles, even giggles—and many participants won't see the point at first. While they're talking, write down the adjectives they use. What's most important is not the specific song, animal or car they pick: it's the reason *why* they picked each one—what they associate with each choice—that will reveal the personality.

At the end of this exercise you'll have a list of adjectives and phrases. If participants share a similar vision, their choices and language will overlap, and clear themes will emerge. If they do not, it may be harder to agree on a list of attributes to define the organization's desired personality, and more discussions may be necessary.

Using Personality to Distinguish

The terms that define the National Military Family Association's personality are *responsive, honest, credible, with gravitas/serious, empowering, patriotic, resilient, a fighter and defender, comprehensive, holistic,* and *grassroots*. Armed with a list of adjectives such as this, an organization's staff can assess the communications materials they produce much more effectively. For example, the National Military Family Association works hard to ensure that its writing is simple and straightforward, not jargony. Its staff want this writing to feel *grassroots* and *honest* to the people who read it. Similarly, the design of this organization's materials features the colors of the American flag, emphasizing the nonprofit's *patriotic* nature.

The personality of Congregation B'nai Jeshurun called forth these terms: *inclusive; progressive; traditional and timeless yet innovative; dynamic, vibrant, inspiring; rabbi-led yet participatory: a community; values-driven; socially conscious and* active; musical; challenging; constantly evolving; personal, human; fun, friendly; joyful; transporting, inspirational; sincere, industrious; content-rich; a bridge; a tapestry; with Kavanah ("intention"). After defining its personality, Congregation B'nai Jeshurun began using images of congregants and activities in its materials to communicate the *inclusive* and *community* aspects of its personality. In its materials, photos are often used together to form a visual tapestry, and they feature not only faces but also images of the synagogue, the Torah, and people dancing.

The personality definitions of both the National Military Family Association and Congregation B'nai Jeshurun include some adjectives that other organizations might also claim, but it is unlikely that many organizations would arrive at the same overall list. Your organization's personality should distinguish it from its peers and shape the tone and style of all its communications.

A Foundation for Everyday Activities

A majority of organizations never fully define all the elements in their Organizational Level. Most commonly, nonprofits consider vision and mission but give little time and attention to values, objectives, audiences, positioning, or personality. These organizations are taking a short-term view. They also tend to review their Organizational Level elements only infrequently, usually during times of significant change or strategic planning. It's as if, during these times, a select few of the Organizational Level elements suddenly stretch and rigorously exercise—only to doze off again once day-to-day operations resume.

Organizations with a long-term point of view tackle their Organizational Level differently. First, they go deeper—articulating values, developing objectives, understanding their audiences, and defining their positioning and personality. These additional layers add depth and dimension by creating a substantive link between the Organizational Level and the Identity Level and Experiential Level.

Informing Day-to-Day Communications

The Organizational Level is the strategic platform that daily communications and all other aspects of the organization's work are built on. The brandraising approach serves as a bridge connecting Organizational Level elements to everyday communications work. For example, it helps staff and board link items such as the newsletter, e-mail campaign, or annual report back to vision and mission.

As the number of staff grows and new departments form, most organizations begin to centralize communications. Instead of allowing staff to produce materials on a catch-as-catch-can basis, the organization becomes clearer about who's responsible for the Identity Level and Experiential Level of communications. To start with, a director of development or chief operating officer might have defined responsibilities for communications listed in his or her job description.

Identifying who's in charge of communications helps to centralize operations and clarify responsibility, but it's just one step in the process. Brandraising requires a well-developed, substantive Organizational Level to provide a framework that can be used to work strategically, rather than reactively or subjectively. Without it, the people who manage communications will be using their intuition and personal points of view to make decisions, rather than the organization's agreed-upon vision, mission, values, objectives, audiences, positioning, and personality.

Use these questions to connect day-to-day communications to the Organizational Level of brandraising:

- Which of these ideas communicates our vision, mission, and values most effectively?
- How does this activity support our objectives?
- Which of these ideas will most likely engage our audiences?
- Which of these ideas best reflects our positioning?
- Which of these ideas best reflects our personality?

Getting Ready to Begin Brandraising at the Organizational Level

Traditionally, organizations start making communications changes for brandraising at the Identity Level or even at the Experiential Level. Revisiting the elements in the Organizational Level, or perhaps defining them for the first time, will make the process longer but will ultimately ensure its long-term success.

These questions will help you determine if the timing is right to begin brandraising in your organization:

- How formally have we considered our vision, mission, values, objectives, audiences, positioning, and personality in the past? Is now the right time to revisit or define these elements?

- Is there general agreement among our leaders about the value of brandraising at the Organizational Level?
- Can our board and staff commit to a process of self-exploration, discovery, and development at this time?

If you opt to move forward, you'll need an experienced person (consultant, staff member, or board member) to guide the process. Typically, work on vision, mission, values, and objectives is directed by a strategic planning professional, and work on audiences, positioning, and personality is more likely to be directed by a marketing or communications-focused professional. Depending on his or her level of experience and point of view and on the culture of your organization, your facilitator will direct a process that may take days, weeks, or months. It will include discussions, drafting your Organizational Level, refining it with input, and building buy-in. Although there is no one right way to do this, here are a few pointers:

- Agree on the process up front and discuss it with board and staff leaders before it begins in order to build understanding and buy-in. The process should reflect your organization's culture and working style (formal, casual, research-driven, or inclusive, for example).
- Be clear about who's expected to do what and by when. Create a calendar with roles clearly defined and assigned and linked to dates.
- Create forums (brainstorming sessions, discussions, online groups, and so forth) where all stakeholders can appropriately share their points of view in a safe, nonjudgmental way.

The end result of this process should be a document that is approved by your nonprofit's leaders and that articulates the organization's vision, mission, values, objectives, audiences, positioning, and personality.

In Summary

- Vision, mission, and values are concepts that must be explored through leadership-level dialogue. Once there is consensus, they can be translated into the statements that are essential to effective communications, but it's important not to get pinned down in details or semantics during development.
- Defining organizational objectives is vital for communications planning too, to ensure that all materials link back to tangible goals. Objectives should also be tied closely to budgets. Successfully achieved objectives signal a mission that has been accomplished.
- Audiences are often oversimplified by broad labels such as *donors, clients*, and *volunteers*. Putting a face, name, and personal characteristics to the label (creating an audience persona) makes it easier to identify what your audiences might be looking for from your organization and how you can communicate with them on more audience-centric terms.
- Positioning and personality are concepts that for-profits have used for years to define the strategy behind their identities and communications overall. Defined positioning and personality can form a useful strategic platform during Identity Level and Experiential Level brandraising.

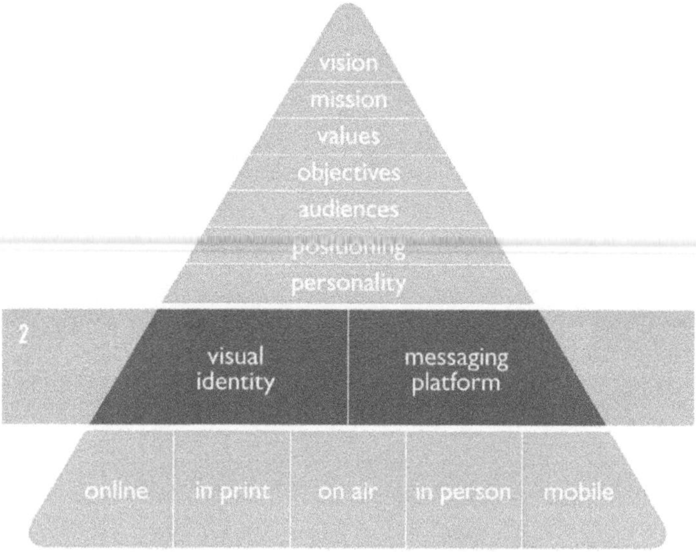
vision
mission
values
objectives
audiences
positioning
personality
2
visual identity
messaging platform
online
in print
on air
in person
mobile

2. IDENTITY LEVEL: What most people think of as *branding*—specifically, the visual identity and messaging platform

CHAPTER 5

Brandraising at the Identity Level

The Identity Level of brandraising deals with two areas—the *visual identity* and the *messaging platform*. Together these areas contain the communications elements most people associate with the term *branding*.

- The visual identity includes the organization's logo (and program logos, if relevant) and also its color palette, typography, imagery (such as photography), and preferred use of graphics.
- The messaging platform includes the organization's name (and program names, if relevant) and also its tagline(s); vision, mission, and values statements; key messages; boilerplate copy; lexicon of terminology; and elevator pitch.

Each of these two areas is worthy of a book unto itself. The goal of this chapter is to provide an overview of their components as a guide for staff people who are managing or developing a nonprofit's visual identity or messaging platform.

For an introduction to the importance of brandraising at the Identity Level, consider the example of one of the most powerful fundraising efforts in recent years: Barack Obama's presidential campaign. Much has already been written about the ways in which this campaign raised half a billion dollars online over twenty-one months. Three million donors made 6.5 million donations, adding up to more than $500 million. Six million of those donations were in increments of $100 or less, and the average online gift was $80—with the average Obama supporter giving more than once. Our new president also raised money the old-fashioned way—offline—but the bulk of the more than $600 million in total support was raised online (Vargas, 2008). That's significantly more than most organizations will ever raise online—and probably offline too.

When you consider the Identity Level of the Obama campaign's brand, what comes to mind? More specifically, what visuals can you recall from the campaign? You might, for instance, think of the color blue, which dominated all communications, or the Obama campaign logo that seemed to be everywhere. Perhaps you think of the famous portrait of Obama's face in red, white, and blue by artist Shepard Fairey. No doubt you saw all of these visuals if you were in the United States during 2008, because they were used extremely consistently and seemed to be everywhere.

Similarly, the Obama campaign was very consistent with its messages. "Yes we can" and "change we can believe in" were phrases we heard so regularly that the postelection cheers of "yes we did" made perfect sense.

The Obama campaign developed a tight brandraising structure that leveraged the candidate's *positioning* as "the candidate for change." The campaign's *personality* was *casual, accessible, new-generation, change-oriented, innovative, stately,* and also *respectful of tradition.* The visual identity and the messaging platform of the campaign worked together to communicate its positioning and personality.

The Visual Identity

Many nonprofit staff people focus on using their organization's logo consistently and overlook the power of other visual elements to communicate. In fact, colors, typography, and artwork (such as photography) can communicate on a deeper, even unconscious, level than a logo can. This happens because most people have feelings, rather than conscious thoughts, about color—and these feelings help to establish or reinforce the organization's desired personality. In the same way, a particular typeface can communicate friendliness, tradition, or grandeur, and do so without being heavy-handed. Thoughtful use of color, type, images, and graphic elements can also establish a sense of consistency and connection between different channels and tools.

Logos

For many, the word *brand* is synonymous with *logo,* because we've all grown up with a basic understanding that logos are emblems, marks, or other graphics designed to communicate about an organization, company, or product. Perhaps this is because the use of logos has been around so much longer than branding or marketing as industries, in the forms of, for example, family crests or cattle branding.

There are three types of logos:

- Logos that use typography only, such as those for Google (Figure 5.1) and for BAM (the Brooklyn Academy of Music, a well-known arts venue; Figure 5.2).
- Logos that alter typography to create a mark within the type, such as the logo for the nonprofit organization inMotion (Figure 5.3).
- Logos that use a visual icon or mark, sometimes called an *ideagram*, such as the logos for the American Red Cross (Figure 5.4) and for the National Military Family Association (Figure 5.5).

FIGURE 5.1 Google Logo

FIGURE 5.2 BAM Logo

inMotion
✝ *Justice for All Women*

FIGURE 5.3 inMotion Logo

FIGURE 5.4 American Red Cross Logo

FIGURE 5.5 National Military Family Association Logo

Logos with Icons or Marks

When the marks used by the March of Dimes, the American Red Cross, the United Way, or the World Wildlife Federation are displayed without their accompanying organization names, most people can still accurately identify each nonprofit. These organizations have used the same marks for so long that they've reached a point of saturation where most Americans, certainly most nonprofit professionals, recognize them instantly.

Visual marks or icons with an organization's name transcend language and literacy barriers, which is valuable when working internationally. For instance, the Red Cross (or Red Crescent in Muslim countries) leverages the power of a simple, clear mark extremely well; one need not read the name to recognize the organization.

The downside of visual marks is that they can easily become cliché, especially in the field of human services. What family-focused or child-focused organization can't use an icon of a small child? What homeless-serving organization wouldn't use a shelter or house? These marks can backfire—creating a look that's so close to the marks of comparable organizations that it's confusing for donors and other audiences.

Logotypes and Acronyms

Logotypes (logos consisting only of typography or of type with some small embellishment, such as the bent staple in the Staples logo) count on the organization's name to communicate first and foremost. They also rely heavily on the selected typeface to communicate personality. If the organization's name is a strong element in its messaging platform, this can be effective. However, it can be problematic when translated into other languages, and some organizations find themselves redesigning their logo as they begin to work internationally.

Acronyms, which are typically shorthand for the organization's name, rarely work effectively in logos. Only audiences who are close to the organization already will understand what the acronym stands for and associate it with the full name. Others will fail to receive the message a name might communicate and may not engage as a result, or they may confuse one organization with another. Some audiences may even feel excluded, as if the organization were only for those in the know.

There are, of course, exceptions. Some organizations use their acronym so consistently and effectively in communications that they build awareness for what it means. These rare nonprofits are usually in the limelight enough that they can leverage media coverage or other forms of visibility to reinforce what their acronym stands for. PETA, for example, which many people know is People for the Ethical Treatment of Animals, has been able to do this effectively because of the high level of media attention it receives.

But why invest limited dollars to raise awareness for an acronym? If your organization has a meaningful name (more on names later in this chapter), getting it out there will help you advance your mission more effectively.

Choosing the Right Kind of Logo

If it's not obvious what type of logo would be most appropriate for your organization, ask your graphic designer to explore a few options in each category (type only, type altered, type and mark). Then use the following questions to facilitate a discussion about these options:

- Which of these logos best reflects our positioning? Why?
- Which of these logos best reflects our personality? Why?

- Which of these logos will be most engaging to our audiences? Why?
- Which of these logos communicates our vision, mission, and values most effectively?

If these questions are starting to sound familiar, that's good. Effective brandraisers regularly revisit these questions and use them to inform decisions. Figure 5.6 shows two logo redesigns that were developed to move the organizations toward a visual identity that better represented their Organizational Level elements.

Typography

The term *typography* was originally coined to describe the study, art, and technique of working with movable type in printing, but today it's also used to describe how styles of type (fonts and sizes) are handled online. Volumes of information, research, and theory inform the development and use of typefaces today, and there are tens of thousands of options to choose from. Books on type theory also abound. (Or, to get a glimpse into the depths of this world, watch the movie *Helvetica*.) The term *font* is often misused: in strict design vernacular a font is a particular style and size of type (for instance, 9 point Arial), whereas the term *typeface* applies to all sizes and styles (italics or bold, for example) of a particular type family.

Typefaces can communicate modernism, tradition, playfulness, formality, informality—a range of attributes that might closely relate to an organization's desired personality. The goal is to select typefaces that do closely

FIGURE 5.6 Logo Redesigns: Before and After Examples

relate to your organization's personality and to use them consistently.

Selecting Typography

People who study type (yes, those people really exist!) have strong ideas about selecting and using typography for maximum impact. Typically, designers select a small number of typefaces when developing visual identities: often, one serif and one sans serif typeface. (A *serif* is the fine line that extends from the tops and bottoms of letters, making them easier to read; a typeface with serifs is usually used for the body text of a book or other copy-intensive publication.) The fewer the number of typefaces used, and the more consistently they are used, the more the organization's materials appear to be consistent.

In an ideal world, all of an organization's materials, even letters, memos, and other correspondence, will use the selected typography (by building the selected type styles into document templates). This sends a subtle but clear message: consistency and quality matter. Your organization's correspondence will then set it apart from the many users of Times and Arial (default typefaces on many computers) and will help readers connect the dots to its other publications.

Using Typography Online

It's hard to control the typefaces audiences see online because they are largely determined by settings on each viewer's local computer. For instance, a Web site designed with Bodoni as the default typeface will be viewed correctly only by people who have Bodoni installed on their computers. For everyone else, the type will default to another more standard selection.

There are two options for building visual consistency across the typography of your e-mails, Web site, and other online communications. Substitute a typeface your audiences are likely to have installed on their computers (for example, Helvetica or Arial for your original sans serif choice and Times for your serif choice), or treat printed documents as artwork by converting them into JPEG or GIF format. Converting type into artwork so it displays consistently online (for example, Gill Sans shows up as Gill Sans no matter who's viewing it) will make it harder for search engines to read the content of the copy and will slow down loading time. For that reason, type as artwork should be used sparingly. On the flip side, using generic typefaces will make your organization feel generic too, which may mean a lost opportunity if you were hoping to stand out from the pack.

To solve this dilemma, most organizations with strong visual identities strike a balance between the two. In print, they use typography that expresses their personalities and differentiates them. Online, they convert key typographical elements, such as their tagline, or occasional headlines, into artwork. If the organization's logo is type only, that, too is treated as artwork so it can't change to a default typeface. For the remainder of each online communication, these organizations opt for the generic typography that is as close to their offline use as possible.

More important than following standards of traditional typography is selecting typefaces that are audience-centric. When communicating with older people, using very small fonts is a sure-fire misstep, for instance. Using hand-drawn looking fonts for anything pertaining to kids can feel clichéd and patronizing. Pick typefaces that reflect your organization's personality but that will also feel identifiable and appropriate to the audiences you're trying to reach.

Color

With the rise of affordable four-color offset and digital printing, not to mention the full-color spectrum available on the Internet and e-mail, it's easier than ever to use color flexibly. However, the strongest, clearest visual identities use a primary and a secondary color palette. An organization's primary palette will contain the one or two colors used in the logo and core materials. Primary palette colors are typically used in stationery, printed newsletters, flyers, and other low-cost printed pieces. An organization's secondary palette will contain colors that work well with the primary colors. These colors are used more decoratively, to add accents and emphasis, particularly online where no additional costs are incurred when colors are added.

Imagine a publication from the Red Cross that featured that organization's logo in pink or orange. Hard to imagine, isn't it? Consistency of color is one of the great hallmarks of a strong visual identity.

Designers and printers frequently refer to color processes such as PMS, CMYK, or RGB. Pantone Matching System (PMS) is a color system used for offset printing. These are custom-mixed colors typically used in one-, two-, or three-color printing runs. Hex and RGB are online color processes in which each color is defined by its combination of red, green, and blue light rays. CMYK is shorthand for cyan, magenta, yellow, and black (the latter represented by the letter *K*), which can be layered together, using screens of dots, to create the illusion of a uniform color. Like PMS, CMYK (also referred to as a *four color*) is a color process used only in offset printing. Look at a magazine under a magnifying glass to see CMYK in action. Tiny cyan, magenta, yellow, and black dots overlap and intersect to create the illusion of lifelike color.

A capable designer will select colors that work well in all formats.

Photographs, Icons, and Other Graphic Elements

Many organizations use photographs, illustrations, or other graphic decorative elements (stripes, icons, dots, and the like) as part of their visual identities. Organizations' use of these elements is often somewhat ad hoc, but approaching them more deliberately can have a significantly positive impact. For instance, an organization striving to communicate a personality that's *reassuring, credible, professional,* and *stable* would use traditional imagery, handled in ways unlikely to challenge the audience. Conversely, an organization with a personality that's *edgy, challenging, smart,* and *unexpected* might use images that employ special filters or effects, unusual crops, or even big, bold type as graphic elements.

Mood Boards

Mood boards are collages, much like posters, that contain a range of images, colors, and perhaps other graphic elements (information visualizations, stripes, textures, icons, and so forth). Before design work on a new visual identity begins, mood boards help the team involved explore what types of visuals will best express the organization's Organizational Level (particularly its personality). This jumpstarts the creative process and helps it proceed smoothly at later stages by providing a visual road map.

A professional graphic designer will develop mood boards in a software program such as PhotoShop or InDesign, using images and other elements found online. Nondesigners can make mood boards by printing images out and then cutting and collaging them onto a piece of poster board. Technique doesn't matter; the point is to create something that helps everyone begin to see the visual identity's future direction.

Through the process of assembling and refining a mood board, members of the creative and management team begin to define a shared sense of what the visual identity should look and feel like. Do the photographs express an unusual point of view? Does the style, cropping, or color reflect the attributes in the Organizational Level personality of the organization?

Because logos are often reviewed out of context, creating mood boards also helps people who aren't able to visualize to easily imagine what their organization's Web site, brochures, and other materials might ultimately look like. As designers create the visual identity, the mood board can be a useful reference tool to make sure an organization's visuals fit its ideas. Figures 5.7 and 5.8 show examples of mood boards created to assist the National Brain Tumor Society and the National Military Family Association as they refined their visual identities.

FIGURE 5.7 Mood Board Developed for the
National Brain Tumor Society

FIGURE 5.8 Mood Board Developed for the
National Military Family Association

The Messaging Platform

Although the elements of a visual identity (particularly logos) are often developed out of context, they are rarely used alone. Logos, for example, are displayed with copy on the cover of a publication, with a tagline on stationery, and with other visuals and copy online. Because audiences experience visuals and messages together at the Experiential Level (covered in detail in the following chapter), these elements should be deliberately developed to complement each other.

If possible, organizations should develop or refine their messaging platform in parallel with their visual identity. Ideally, designers working on visuals will collaborate with writers working on messages in order to ensure that all elements fit together to form a cohesive whole. For example, because an organization's name, logo, and tagline will often be viewed together, it makes sense to write the tagline with an understanding of what the visuals (logo, color, and typography) will express.

As outlined earlier, the messaging platform, often called the *written brand*, includes the name of the organization and its programs; tagline(s); vision, mission, and values statements; key messages; boilerplate; an elevator pitch; and, for some nonprofits, a lexicon. Here are brief definitions of each element, with fuller discussions in the sections that follow:

NAMES: The organization's name and the names of its programs—and how they are abbreviated or adapted in informal contexts or in formal writing after the initial use of the full name—communicate volumes.

TAGLINES: Taglines succinctly communicate the organization's positioning, typically in fewer than eight words, and appear graphically in formal organization communications.

VISION, MISSION, AND VALUES STATEMENTS: Formally written and board-approved statements used in print and online, often verbatim. (Vision, mission, and values were discussed in Chapter Four.)

KEY MESSAGES: Central ideas that must be communicated in order to articulate the organization's positioning. Typically, organizations will have at least three and no more than ten key messages, backed up by supporting points.

BOILERPLATE: Standardized copy used by an organization, along with its mission statement, to express its personality and positioning while communicating its key messages. Boilerplate may often serve as *about us* copy, or at the bottom of a press release, for instance.

ELEVATOR PITCH: Two or three sentences that express the essence of the organization's positioning. Ideally, all ambassadors or spokespeople for the organization have memorized the elevator pitch and can recite it verbatim.

LEXICON: A list of definitions of words and phrases, sometimes developed by organizations in sectors that use jargon extensively or problematically to help them translate *industry-speak* into more audience-centric language.

Not every organization will develop all of these elements in a messaging platform. For instance, some organizations develop mission statements but leave their vision and values as concepts that inform the organization's work rather than formalizing them in writing. Others find it unnecessary to develop boilerplate and use their mission statements instead. Some nonprofits find it easy to explain what they do in audience-centric terms and forgo developing a lexicon. There is no single correct approach. What's most important is that your organization develops a messaging platform that can serve as a clear and useful basis for any writing or speaking its members do.

Staff refer to messaging platforms at the start of any major writing or external communications project (a brochure or annual report, Web site copy, a press release, or a speech for an event, for example). Always referring to the same points and using the same language may seem dull and repetitious to the staff, but it weaves a consistent, cohesive experience for audiences—one that reinforces the ideas of the Organizational Level. By avoiding beginning with a blank piece of paper each time, writers may also work faster and with more consistency.

Names

As with all types of businesses, nonprofit names run the gamut. Some are no-nonsense and straightforward (the Brooklyn Community Foundation and New York City Charter School Center), some are aspirational (Doctors Without Borders, Safe Horizon), and some are change oriented (Partnership for a Drug-Free America, Save the Children). Organizational names are one of the first places accidental branding is evident, because most founders select a name before they've had time to consider the long view (accidental branding and taking the long view were

TABLE 5.1 Three Organizations That Changed Their Names

Original or Previous Name	New Name
NOW Legal Defense Fund	Legal Momentum
Victim Services	Safe Horizon
Center for Children + Families	SafeSpace

explored in Chapter Two). Yet a name is often the first and most widely traveled ambassador for any organization or for a key program.

Table 5.1 offers three examples of organizations that changed their names in order to communicate more effectively. In many cases, names are changed to move away from jargon or confusing or dated terms and toward something more aspirational and change oriented.

Pros and Cons of Name Changing

Changing an organization's name is a difficult process. It requires planning, preparation, changes to articles of incorporation or other legal documents, the expense of updating documents, and a long process of educating audiences about the change. Audiences become familiar with—and often attached to—an organization's name, whether it's effective or not. Although it's rare to find an organization that truly loves its name, most feel they've developed real equity over time that they'd lose were they to change it.

Weighing whether or not a name change is a good idea is hard to do without a proposed new name to consider against the existing name; most people will simply respond with a no when faced with the possibility of change.

Rather than asking, "Should we change our name?" I suggest starting by asking this: "If we were starting the organization today, what name would we select to express our Organizational Level?" Brainstorm possible names with staff, volunteers, and other insiders. The brainstorming process involves no commitment to change the name—it's just an exploration. If a strong option emerges from the brainstorming process, then leaders can weigh the merits of the new name against the risks of losing the equity of the current name. In some cases this leads to adjustments to the current name rather than a wholesale change.

There's no right or wrong way to explore new names. There's also no one-size-fits-all solution when it comes to names: an aspirational name with a straightforward tagline (such as Robin Hood Foundation: Targeting Poverty in New York City) can be highly effective. Conversely, a straightforward name can be augmented by a tagline that adds hope, humor, or a rallying cry (such as Foundation for Jewish Camp: Community by the Cabinful).

Acronyms, Abbreviations, and Colloquial Usage

Many for-profit businesses have successfully used acronyms instead of their full names. People over age forty generally know that IBM stands for International Business Machines. Those who are under forty might not know that, but they certainly do know IBM's positioning as a leader in the computer and technology field. A similar statement might be made for UPS (United Parcel Service). Both IBM and UPS benefit from longevity, reach, and big advertising budgets, all of which help to ensure name recognition—whether a full name or an acronym.

But do you know what BCF stands for? On the one hand, if you live in Baltimore, you might think of the Baltimore Community Foundation. New Yorkers, on the other hand, might think of the Brooklyn Community Foundation. Others will think of the Black College Fund. Or maybe you're a member of the Barbados Chess Foundation? The Web site www.acronymfinder.com lets you type in any acronym and see how many businesses and organizations it already represents (when I looked, I found thirty-nine listed for BCF alone!). The point is, an acronym is meaningful only for the people close enough to the organization to know what it stands for.

When developing a name, consider what abbreviated form your staff and board members should use when speaking or writing informally. I recommend avoiding acronyms whenever possible, and abbreviating to something that adds more content. For example, rather than abbreviate National Military Family Association to NMFA, use "the Association" when referring to it colloquially. Wherever possible, use the full name (even when that seems heavy-handed to you) to build and reinforce name recognition. The same holds true when raising visibility for key programs or issues. Staff people at Parent Project Muscular Dystrophy, for example, don't refer to Duchenne muscular dystrophy as DMD, they refer to it as Duchenne, which helps bring visibility to this little-known genetic disorder.

There are rare exceptions to these guidelines. In 2008, the United Negro College Fund announced that it would change its name to UNCF but retain its well-known tagline, "A mind is a terrible thing to waste." This change overcame the barrier presented by a name that is no longer politically correct, but leveraged the equity of the organization's terrific tagline to help ensure that UNCF is recognized as the same organization as the United Negro College Fund.

Taglines

When well written, a tagline can add enormous value and clarity to a lackluster organization or program name. It can also add specificity and clarity to a name that's abstract or aspirational. From a fundraising point of view, a tagline can focus distracted donors on the essence of your nonprofit's work. The for-profit world has used taglines effectively for decades, and now many nonprofits are learning from their example.

- UNCF: A mind is a terrible thing to waste.
- Cancer Research Institute: Advancing Immunology. Conquering Cancer.
- Historic Entertainment: Join for the swords. Stay for the friends.
- AmeriCares: A passion to help. The ability to deliver.
- Foundation for Jewish Camp: Community by the Cabinful
- Women's Sports Foundation: Equal Play.

Conversely, a weak tagline can reinforce poor or fuzzy associations. Many organizations in the health sector have taglines along the lines of "research • education • advocacy" or "research • treatment • change," for instance. Even though these taglines communicate something about an organization's work, they lack the unique language or terms that help us understand exactly what makes the group tick, and why it is different from others in its space.

What does a great tagline provide? Personality and positioning. A great tagline communicates something of the organization's culture and tone. It can also make claims or take positions that set the organization apart from other organizations in its space.

Creating Your Tagline

Ideally, you'd hire a talented, experienced writer to develop tagline options for your nonprofit. If your budget doesn't allow this, you might approach this project by forming a working committee to develop and solicit tagline ideas. But proceed with caution: you are likely to get what you pay for. It's hard to synthesize all of the variables that make a tagline work into two to eight words—and especially hard for people who are very close to the organization. Whether you hire professionals to help or do it internally, it will be much easier to define what your tagline should communicate once your Organizational Level is in place.

Remember also that most taglines will be viewed only as they accompany the organization's name, not as text. For instance, a tagline is often seen at the top of a Web site's home page, on the front or back cover of a printed piece, or in a letterhead but rarely appears in the body text of a grant application or a letter to a donor. Although a great tagline should make sense as text, it's most essential that the tagline works visually when used with an organization's name and logo. Some organizations find that taglines are most effectively developed after they've finalized their name and logo. For organizations that are tackling their visual identity and messaging platform in tandem, with one creative team, collaboration between the logo designer and the writers who are developing messages can spark unexpected creative solutions.

Assessing Your Tagline

Put your nonprofit's tagline to the test:

- Make a list of all the organizations that your non-profit collaborates or competes with. This list might include agencies with programs reaching the same audiences you serve or organizations your funders also support.
- Write your current or proposed tagline in large letters at the top of the list.
- Read each organization's name, followed by *your* tagline. Does your tagline work for other organizations? One or two others or many others?

The fewer organizations that could use your tagline, the more unique it may be, and the more likely it is to express your organization's positioning and personality well.

Vision, Mission, and Values Statements

Chapter Four covered organizational vision, mission, and values in depth. Vision, mission, and values statements are the way these ideas are written down so they can be broadly shared. Writing these statements requires painstaking attention to language and building buy-in to ensure that they're used verbatim once approved by the executive director and board.

Because vision, mission, and values statements are for public consumption, they must be written clearly, comprehensibly, and in a manner that reflects the organization's personality and positioning. When staff people feel close to these ideas, they will often find writing them out concisely difficult and may add too much detail or use jargon excessively. In these cases an outside writer, ideally a professional with nonprofit experience, might edit the language to make it work.

Key Messages

Key messages are the ideas that an organization must express in order to establish its positioning in the minds of its audiences. For instance, if an organization's positioning statement describes that organization as the leading resource for a community or issue, then the key messages must clearly establish and justify that leadership position. Media-savvy organizations and politicians have used key messages for decades to keep their spokespeople on message.

Here, for example, are the key messages used by the National Brain Tumor Society:

CENTRAL RESOURCE. We are the 'go-to' organization for all things brain tumor related.

RESEARCH. We invest wisely and deeply in innovative research that will lead to advances and ultimately to a cure.

PATIENT SERVICES. We offer top-notch resources and caring support for everyone affected by brain tumors.

COLLABORATION. We are inclusive in our efforts to find a cure and to provide the best patient services possible.

ABOUT BRAIN TUMORS. A brain tumor is a mass of abnormal tissue cells that multiply uncontrollably, taking up space within the skull and interfering with normal brain activity.

Key messages should be woven into everything written by your nonprofit organization. They should be written down in your organization's style guide, but not listed in any public-facing communications. For example, a visitor to your Web site won't find them under a "Key Messages" heading but will experience them as they are woven throughout the copy in multiple places on that site.

Key messages can be developed in a number of ways. Some organizations facilitate meetings with key stakeholders (including the staff, volunteers, members, and the board) to discuss the essence of what the organization is and does, using an iterative process to narrow options down to the point where they are concise but not oversimplified. Other organizations engage external consultants to develop their key messages or to facilitate an internal process.

When developing key messages internally, begin by asking this question, "What messages must be communicated in order to establish our positioning in our audiences' minds?" Nonprofits often want to develop many messages—but try to resist this urge. Key messages should be big ideas. Back them up with examples or other nitty-gritty when you can, but don't front-load them too much. You'll be asking people to remember and use these messages regularly and having too many will make using them cumbersome and likely to be ignored by the people you most want to have repeating them.

Boilerplate

Once an organization's key messages are finalized, it might also develop generic, audience-centric boilerplate copy that wraps the messages up into a brief paragraph or two that can be paired with the mission statement to provide a comprehensive overview. Exhibit 5.1 contains the actual

---

EXHIBIT 5.1 Example of National Brain Tumor Society's Boilerplate, with Mission Statement

Boilerplate Using Key Messages

National Brain Tumor Society is a leader in the brain tumor community, bringing together the best of research and patient services to be a comprehensive resource for patients, families, caregivers, researchers, and medical professionals.

We invest wisely and deeply across the research spectrum, seeking new therapeutic targets and improving existing treatments, which will ultimately lead to a cure. Our staff and advisory team encourage research that connects directly to patient care and enhances quality of life for all brain tumor patients.

National Brain Tumor Society offers top-notch resources and caring support for everyone affected by brain tumors, including those that have lost a loved one. We provide education and information to help patients, families, and caregivers make informed decisions and develop strong support systems during every stage of the journey—from diagnosis through treatment to end of care, and beyond.

Mission Statement

National Brain Tumor Society is a nonprofit organization inspiring hope and providing leadership within the brain tumor community. We exist to find a cure and improve the quality of life for those affected by brain tumors. We fund strategic research, deliver support services, and promote collaboration.

---

boilerplate developed for the National Brain Tumor Society, using the key messages outlined earlier. This boilerplate can stand alone (for instance, on the bottom of a press release) or be used with the organization's mission statement.

The Elevator Pitch

You find yourself in an elevator with a potential donor who asks you what your organization does. You have time only for a one- or two-sentence description of the organization, in general, easy-to-digest terms. If your organization has prepared an elevator pitch, you know exactly what to say. Ideally, every staff and board member will know the pitch by heart and be able to repeat it verbatim when asked about the organization (whether they're in the elevator or not). If they don't memorize the pitch, leaders should at least be confident that they have its gist (training, which will be covered later in this chapter, is critical). A strong elevator pitch communicates, in the time of an elevator ride, the essence of a nonprofit's Organizational Level: why the nonprofit exists and why it's worth supporting, ideally communicated in a tone and style that demonstrates its personality. Exhibit 5.2 displays the National Brain Tumor

EXHIBIT 5.2 National Brain Tumor Society's Elevator Pitch

The National Brain Tumor Society brings together the best in brain tumor research and supportive patient services. We provide hope to patients, families, and caregivers during every stage of the journey— from diagnosis through treatment and end of care.

Society's elevator pitch. It doesn't use all the key messages because time is too limited. Nor does it offer the level of detail about the organization's work provided in the mission statement. Instead, it boils the major ideas down even further, into two sentences.

The Lexicon

A lexicon is an extremely useful tool for organizations that need to remove jargon from communications so their audiences can understand them better, and for organizations that prefer to use politically correct or more sensitive language. The lexicon is an internal document used to help staff stay on message and to articulate the values of the organization. Exhibit 5.3 is an excerpt from the lexicon of Osborne Association, a New York City human services organization that transforms the lives of people involved with the criminal justice system.

A lexicon can be developed internally by asking staff to develop a list of jargon and other terms they'd like to avoid, and then to supply the terms that might communicate the same ideas in simpler or better language for the layperson. It can be helpful to have someone who's not as close as staff to the organization's work (a volunteer or donor perhaps) suggest language that's more audience-centric.

Building the Messaging Platform

Many organizations enlist the talents of staff or volunteers to help develop or refine the messaging platform. Others turn to freelancers, agencies, and even grantmakers like the Taproot Foundation (www.taprootfoundation.org), which

EXHIBIT 5.3 Excerpt from the Osborne Association's Lexicon

The Osborne Association should use positive language whenever possible. Rather than using the language of law enforcement (which tends to define people by their crimes), we use language that defines people by their strengths. Rather than describing people in terms of their worst action, we describe people by their best selves and greatest potential. We always avoid terms that dehumanize.

Negative Language to Avoid	Positive Language to Use
Offender	Person in conflict with the law
Ex-offender	Formerly incarcerated
Children at-risk	Children experiencing poverty
	Children of the incarcerated
	Children of promise
Victim/survivor	Person harmed by crime
Speaking in deficits, risks	Speaking in strengths
Came from a broken home	Experienced separation from parents

matches skilled volunteers with nonprofits that need creative work done pro bono.

Some messaging platform elements will be easier to develop in-house than others. As noted earlier, developing vision, mission, and values statements and lexicons in-house may make sense—because the meanings of certain words will be ripe with nuance for the staff person who deals with them daily but have much less significance for a professional copywriter. Conversely, a name, a tagline, and key messages are typically harder for staff people to develop, because creating these elements requires an objective and hierarchical view of the organization's work to determine what must be included and what can be omitted.

Sub-Brands

As organizations grow they often launch new programs with separate visual identities and messaging platforms. Unless the audiences for Program A are entirely different from (and want to distance themselves from) those for Program B, the benefits of this approach can be outweighed by the problems it creates. From a fundraising point of view, it makes more sense to link all programs to the organization's *master brand*, so donors who read about Program A associate it with the organization rather than seeing it as a freestanding project. From a program point of view, many of the participants in Program A might also benefit from Program B, so why not help them understand the connection?

Whenever possible, connect the names of programs to the organization itself, and avoid developing visual identities or messaging platforms that distract audiences from connecting with the organization through the program. Figure 5.9 shows how the National Brain Tumor Foundation's logo and tagline relate to its three event-specific sub-brands through typography and mark. (They also relate through color, indicated in this figure by shading.)

National Brain Tumor Society

Leading through research and support

 Ride for Research

New England unites to fight brain tumors

 Brain Tumor Walk

Bay Area unites to fight brain tumors

 Race for Hope

San Francisco unites to fight brain tumors

FIGURE 5.9 Linking Sub-Brands to Main Identity Through Mark and Typography

Integrating the Identity

A style guide and training will help your organization ensure that its visual identity and messaging platform are effectively integrated into its day-to-day communications.

The Style Guide

A style guide is a document created by the same people (outside agency personnel, freelancers, volunteers, or staff members) who developed the organization's visual identity and messaging platform. It captures the important details of an organization's Identity Level elements and makes them easy to reference and use consistently. A useful style guide defines the rules that must be followed to ensure the Identity Level elements are used consistently (for instance, it specifies how to abbreviate the organization's name).

Style guides are the key to building institutional memory and ensuring that new staff people and board members get up to speed fast with the details of how to create and use an organization's Identity Level communications.

A style guide may include

- The organization's positioning and personality statements
- The names, titles, and contact information of those responsible for managing and approving communications
- The processes for developing communications
- The organization's vision, mission, and values statements
- The ways in which the organization's logo may or may not be used
- The ways in which the tagline may or may not be used
- The primary and secondary color palettes
- The typography that is to be used in print and online
- The ways in which photography and other supportive graphic elements (such as illustrations or icons) should be used
- The key messages, with supporting, or backup, points
- The boilerplate copy
- The elevator pitch

- The lexicon
- The locations on the server of the files staff will need

Style guides are useful because they formalize the visual identity, messaging platform, and relevant processes in a document that can be easily referenced. I'm a fan of style guides that are light on text and heavy on visuals so they're easy to scan and find what you need quickly. It's not imperative to show how every possible use of the brand might work. It's much more important for the guide to outline the key ingredients so staff can create their own recipes (that is, communications) and have those communications come out consistently.

Style guides are usually the turf of the director of communications in larger organizations, the director of development in organizations where there is no dedicated communications staff, or the executive director in very small nonprofits. Review your style guide on an annual basis and update it with any necessary changes so it remains relevant.

Training

Training is helpful to ensure that staff, leadership, and other spokespeople use the messaging platform when writing or speaking and that they understand how to use the visual identity when managing or designing materials. It's also the best way to build institutional memory, buy-in, and ownership for Identity Level communications. Training provides a context for the work overall, helps staff and board members understand how to use the brand (and how it applies specifically to their role), and inspires them to maintain it.

Typically, training is conducted using the organization's style guide for reference. The people who created the visual identity and messaging platform typically lead the training. Although specific training sessions might be for board members only, staff only, or both groups together, it's important that both the staff and the board receive appropriate training that builds buy-in and familiarity because, formally or informally, they will serve as representatives of the organization.

Training can cover

- Why the organization undertook brandraising in the first place, and what it hopes to achieve from this change and new approach
- What positioning and personality are, and how these concepts relate to each person's everyday work as a staff or board member of the nonprofit
- How to use the visual identity and messaging platforms
- Whom to go to when people have questions, encounter problems, or need help in using the new Identity

Using Messaging Cheat Sheets

Some staff and board members find it particularly useful to carry around small cards, similar to business cards, that have the nonprofit's mission statement, elevator pitch, and perhaps key messages on them. These "cheat sheets" are most helpful when given to people who've attended training, so they know how to use them.

Identifying Key People to Train

In order to communicate effectively on behalf of the organization, everyone on the staff will need a copy of the style guide and basic training, at a minimum. It's optimal to go even deeper with certain individuals. Here are a few suggestions for basic training:

- *Point-of-entry staff* (receptionists, intake caseworkers, and so forth). Spend time discussing the personality of the organization and how these individuals can convey it given their uniquely visible role as a first point of contact. Role-playing can be a useful way to identify phrases staffers might use to express the organization's mission, positioning, and personality well.
- *Board members.* Board members who serve as spokespeople on a regular basis may benefit from a more personalized, one-on-one discussion of how they can use the Organizational and Identity Levels when they represent the organization. Role-playing can help them get comfortable with using the messaging platform.
- *Staff spokespeople.* Often, the executive director or other chief officer serves as the public spokesperson for the organization. She or he is the one called on to comment to the media, testify during legislative hearings, lead press conferences, and more. If budget allows, it's beneficial to provide this person with professional media training in addition to intensive training on the visual identity and messaging platform elements. Effective media training (ideally, conducted by a media relations and training specialist with deep nonprofit experience) will prepare a spokesperson to be clear, articulate, confident, and on-message when speaking publicly.
- *Celebrities and other ambassadors.* Training celebrities to stay on message can be challenging, but worth it.

Many celebrities have publicists who are important gatekeepers. A closed-door discussion between the executive director, celebrity, and his or her publicist, using the messaging cheat sheet (typically including the mission statement, elevator pitch, and key messages), can help.

In Summary

- The Identity Level is composed of the visual identity (logo, colors, typography, photos, and other graphic elements) and messaging platform (names; tagline[s]; vision, mission, and values statements; key messages; boilerplate; and lexicon).
- Not all organizations formally develop all of these elements when they update or create their Identity Level.
- The Identity Level contains the elements that are hardest to develop without outside help from professional writers or graphic designers.
- Once finalized, these elements must become institutionalized, through the development of a style guide and by training key internal stakeholders and spokespeople.

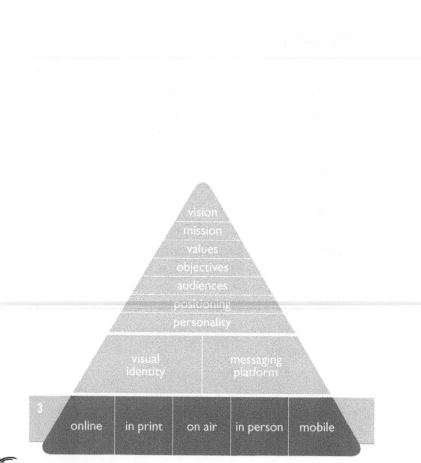

3. EXPERIENTIAL LEVEL: The channels and tools through which audiences connect with the organization

CHAPTER 6

Brandraising at the Experiential Level

If you've devoted your career to making the world a better place, it's easy to be cynical of the for-profit world's deep focus on and investment in marketing. Some for-profits invest heavily in marketing and communications even before they've developed a substantive product to back up those messages. Even though great advertising, extensive media exposure, or a well-known celebrity might increase a nonprofit's visibility, there's no argument that substantive, effective programs must be in place first and foremost. Once they are, then the question is, *How do you reach the clients, donors, policymakers, or media you want to engage in order to fulfill your mission?* How is your organization discovered, understood, and experienced from a donor's, client's, journalist's, or policymaker's point of view? This question must be visited again and again as you strategize, plan, and execute communications, no matter what channels you use.

In the pages that follow, we'll take a look at the most common ways organizations communicate online, in print, in person, on air, and via mobile phones; and explore some of the changes that have taken place recently in these channels. But don't get caught up exclusively in channels and forget about the human experience. To communicate effectively, you need to be thinking of both.

Selecting Audience-Centric Channels

Although individuals have different motivations for engaging with a nonprofit, there are a limited number of channels they can connect through. They can engage *online, in print, in person, on air*, or *by mobile phone*. They are how audiences experience and interact with your organization firsthand.

With that said, it's easy to get caught up in the channels and forget about the human experience. The people you're communicating with will relate to your organization within the contexts of their lives. Instead of fully focusing on your newsletter or Web site, they'll probably skim it with, for example, the TV on in the background, alongside other pieces of mail, with other Web sites tabbed up, in a stack of reports they've been asked to review (perhaps during their morning commute), or on their BlackBerry. Effective brandraising requires maintaining an audience-centric point of view as you select the channels and tools you'll use.

To determine the best ways to reach your audiences on their own terms, develop a survey using Survey Monkey (www.surveymonkey.com), Zoomerang (www.zoomerang.-

com), or another free or low-cost online tool, then embed the survey on your Web site's home page and e-mail it to your house file. Ask multiple-choice questions such as

- How did you originally find out about us? (Possible answer choices: referred by a friend, Web search, mailing, and so forth.)
- Have you received or reviewed any of the following communications from us over the past month? (Possible answer choices: Web site, e-mail, newsletter, mailing, and so forth.)

Keep the questions minimal and the options clear and free of jargon. This survey will provide only a glimpse into the habits and preferences of those you reach digitally, but it can still offer a few useful insights that you can follow up on during conversations, interviews, or focus groups.

How Donors and Prospects Experience You

How do would-be donors (also known as *prospects*) find out about your organization? Do they hear about it from a board member? Receive a direct-mail solicitation? Read about it in the press? See its name mentioned in a friend's Twitter feed? Attend its gala as a guest? Find it through GuideStar, the Wise Giving Alliance, or another source?

When they want to learn more, do they sign up for your organization's newsletter? Request its annual report? Join its Facebook group? Call and ask for more information?

All of these *points of entry* are viable and potentially valuable. The art of building relationships with donors comes in how you engage them once they connect.

Map out how a few of the donors you know well originally connected with your organization, and what communications helped establish their current level of commitment. For example, if they met your organization through their friend who is on the board but what really sealed their commitment was the tour of your agency's programs, then it's clear that your in-person communications are probably an important donor channel.

It's easy to imagine how donors or prospects might learn about your organization but perhaps harder to imagine how they might feel. For instance, are they hesitant about getting involved or being asked for a gift? Delighted to have finally found you? Willing to help as long as you don't ask too much?

It's not realistic, of course, to ask every donor what he or she would like from a relationship with your nonprofit, but it is possible to ask a select few. Take the time to ask donors how they feel and how they'd like you to communicate with them. You'll gain deeper trust and support when your organization listens and delivers.

How Clients Experience Your Organization

A client's point of view will vary enormously depending on the organization's mission, of course. Do your clients hear about your programs through word-of-mouth? By receiving a flyer or other printed piece? By referral from another agency or a friend? When clients or participants come in for programs and services, do you hand out a brochure or flyer that describes your organization or the specific program? Is there signage on the wall that tells them where they are and what the organization does? Do they speak with a staff person who explains what the organization is and does before they dive into an activity?

In 2008, the staff of East River Development Alliance (a human services agency serving several public housing developments in Queens, New York) noted that the community it existed to serve wasn't fully using its free services. Instead, other neighborhood residents, perhaps those with less need, were coming in. East River Development Alliance was marketing aggressively: handing out flyers, advertising, even offering financial incentives to get people to come in for their programs. The programs themselves were outstanding: staff, former clients, and others told story after story of individuals whose lives had been successfully transformed by this organization's great work. So why weren't the people most in need coming in for services?

Informal focus groups at local community centers revealed that many people were familiar with the organization's name and programs, but they were also skeptical about some of the claims the organization made in its materials. "Helping me with my taxes for free? There's got to be a catch in there someplace," one person said, "you don't get something for nothing in this neighborhood." These informal focus groups (five of them in all) revealed that the East River Development Alliance could do a better job of reaching out by telling the stories of the people who'd benefited from its programs and by using word-of-mouth in the community. Instead of producing postcards emphasizing getting things for free, it should organize an event for program graduates and their friends at which they could discuss the value of the services they had received. The organization shifted its marketing approach to these new strategies, channels, and tools, and almost immediately saw an increase in program participation by members of the community it aims to serve.

Reaching clients optimally may also mean offering programs after hours or on weekends, having bilingual staff, or simply installing signs that help people find the bathroom without having to ask. It may also mean adjusting the reading level of program and other materials up or down, making type larger, or greeting everyone who walks into the office with an open smile.

Many people, particular clients who come in for social services, experience anxiety in new situations. Communications that help them feel at home, understand your organization, and learn what they can expect from you may be the most important place to start.

How the Media Experience Your Organization

How does a journalist, blogger, or other member of the media connect with your organization? Do they find it online when researching a story? Through a press release staff have sent? By reading about its work on a popular blog? By hearing about it through other people they're interviewing? When they visit your Web site to check your organization out, can they easily find its mission statement? Do they visit the site's online *press room*? When they call your organization, are they immediately connected to an appointed spokesperson? Does that person's voice-mail include a cell phone number so the spokesperson can be easily reached when he or she doesn't answer?

More than other audiences, the media rely on very specific channels of communication. First and foremost, your organization's Web site (particularly its press room area) should provide the core information media personnel need to understand the organization's work and whom to contact. Press releases (usually sent via e-mail or through services) and press conferences are also critical outreach channels for journalists.

Journalists and, increasingly, bloggers are usually busy people looking for credible information fast. If they can't find what they're looking for quickly on your site or don't connect with a helpful individual the first time they reach out, they're likely to move on and seek the information they need elsewhere. They also don't like to receive information that's not directly related to the beat they cover.

How Policymakers Experience Your Organization

Perhaps a legislative assistant or congressional staff person is researching a topic relevant to your organization's work. Will these people find your organization easily if they search online? Will they recall your nonprofit's recent e-mail campaign? Or hear about the organization from their constituents or colleagues on the Hill? When they visit your organization's Web site, is the content they need easily accessible? Is it easy to find contact information if they want to speak to the executive director or another senior staff person? When they call, are they immediately connected to the right person?

Policymakers and their staffs may be the least likely audience to proactively come looking for your organization. Most often, they connect to organizations because someone—their constituents, your staff, a consultant, or a respected peer—reaches out and engages them. They're looking for credible resources: individuals who have the credentials to speak reliably on behalf of an issue. Often, these individuals will be program staff or grassroots representatives who speak from experience as *insiders*.

Embedding Your Organization in Its Audience

During wartime, journalists embed themselves with troops to deepen their understanding and thus their ability to report. There's no better way to get to know a subject than to be immersed in it. Consider devoting a week to getting to know your audiences' communications habits and preferences a bit better. If you're a development person, perhaps you'll spend that week researching your corporate, foundation, or individual supporters' point of view. If you're a program person, you'll want to focus on your clients' opinions. And so on.

If they'll allow you to, spend a few hours shadowing several representative people on a typical day. Observe their usual activities rather than engaging with them. During your time as their shadow, take notes on

- How much time they spend on the phone, in meetings, online, reading, texting, and so forth
- How much information they manage: are they multitaskers juggling lots of information and responding or acting in real time? Or are they more likely to read, file, and move methodically through the tasks at hand?
- Do they use Twitter, Facebook, or other social networking tools regularly?

- Do they seem particularly comfortable or uncomfortable with certain types of communications? Do they prefer to pick up the phone or to chat face-to-face, or are they more likely to text, instant message, or e-mail someone?
- What do they do with the information they receive? Do they file it? Discard it? Share it with a friend or colleague?

At the end of your observation period, it may be helpful to chat with each person about how typical what you saw was for him or her, and what each one would like your organization to consider when communicating.

This exercise can be adapted into a brief survey if spending time in the field proves unrealistic. But you'll gain a much truer sense of your audiences if you can get a firsthand feeling for their lives, rather than asking them to parse their activities intellectually and consciously for you.

At the end of your week of research, write up the findings and share them with others on your staff. You might even write up audience personas (outlined in Chapter Four) based on the people you studied, as a means of using or referring your findings later. Your organization may find it valuable if you talk about your research and findings in a staff meeting:

- What surprised you most about this audience's lifestyle and communications preferences?
- What surprised you least?
- Which experiential channels might be most effective for reaching them?

- Which experiential channels might be least effective?
- What do you think everyone in your organization should keep in mind when communicating with these audiences?

Online

There is growing overlap between the online and the on-air channels, which I'll describe later on. For now, I'll focus on these channels separately. Consider the following online tools:

- Web sites
- E-mails (HTML, text-only, viral)
- Blogs, message boards, listservs, and other interactive and user-generated (*U-gen*) content
- Webinars
- Social networks (LinkedIn, Facebook, MySpace, Changents, Eons, and so forth)
- Social media and aggregators (Twitter, Delicious, Digg, FriendFeed, RSS feeds, and so forth)
- Pay-per-click, banner ads, and other online advertising or marketing
- Virtual worlds (such as Second Life)

Every few months, new ways to connect and engage online seem to emerge. In this section, we'll take a look at the tools nonprofits are regularly using.

Getting into Web 2.0

In the late 1990s, most nonprofits built their first Web sites. The sites were small, not very interactive, and essentially restated the information you might find in a brochure. Some of these Web sites had the ability to accept donations online or perhaps used a content management system so staff could make updates, but rarely did nonprofits build Web sites that served as program tools or used interactive features.

Man, oh man, have times changed. Today nonprofits hold events in virtual worlds, have staff whose full-time job is to monitor the blogosphere, build and maintain their own online communities, and more. *Web 2.0* is a term coined to describe the World Wide Web in its current interactive form, the form most of us have come to expect online today. Rather than read and view static pages, we expect to be able to comment, share our point of view, and be heard.

Over the past few years, even the smallest nonprofits have been coming to terms with online jargon like *Web 2.0*, *user-generated content*, and *social media*, and trying to figure out how to leverage these tools, especially if they're trying to reach people in their thirties and younger. What should a nonprofit make of Facebook? Twitter? LinkedIn? YouTube? Flickr? The challenge many organizations overlook is staffing for this interactivity—most of these tools require staff to monitor and support them on a daily basis.

If you or members of your staff are completely lost during discussions of social media, social fundraising, or Web 2.0, never fear. A number of great resources have emerged to help. Start by viewing some of the excellent instructional videos created by Common Craft (viewable at www.commoncraft.com/show). These short videos explain podcasting, social bookmarking, Twitter, and other new media in short, simple terms that just about anyone can understand. It may even make sense to play a few of these videos at your next staff meeting.

Beth Kanter is a leading consultant on using social media in the nonprofit sector. Her excellent blog, called "Beth's Blog: How Nonprofits Can Use Social Media," covers just about all things regarding new media. (Subscribe to it at http://beth.typepad.com.)

Charlene Li and Josh Bernoff's excellent book *Groundswell: Winning in a World Transformed by Social Technologies*, is a terrific primer. They also blog (at http://blogs.forrester.com/groundswell).

Lastly, a membership organization called NTEN: The Nonprofit Technology Network, offers terrific Webinars, training curricula, and other tools for nonprofit staff people at all levels (start browsing at www.nten.org). NTEN's We Are Media project (www.wearemedia.org) is chock-full of useful social media content. It's a community intended to be a "social media starter kit" for nonprofits, and it's good stuff.

Relevance for Your Nonprofit

Is keeping up with all of this emerging online technology and interactivity necessary for your organization? How do you decide? And how do you determine where to invest your (potentially small) online budget?

Let's go back to the Organizational Level of your organization's communications, and ask a few questions:

- Is communicating online, especially in newer forums like social networking or community sites, consistent with the values and objectives of your organization? Is it consistent with the organization's personality?

- Where are your audiences spending time online now? Would having a presence in those places (for example, Facebook) be an opportunity for your nonprofit to deepen its relationships with key audiences?
- Would social media support your organization's goal positioning, and help it differentiate itself from its peers?
- Does your organization have the staff to monitor the conversations that will occur, develop meaningful content, and manage it all well?

An organization with wired audiences, especially an organization that is striving to communicate a position that reflects leadership and a personality that includes attributes like *state of the art* or *innovative,* is more likely than more traditional groups to monitor and employ online best practices, tools, and new media.

With the rapid changes happening online, it's possible that your organization will overhaul its Web site every two or three years, or that online communities you wouldn't consider now might be central to how you communicate later as your audiences emerge there. Depending on your organization's size and mission, it may even decide to staff up with people devoted exclusively to social media. Today more and more organizations are planning or actually creating vibrant e-mail campaigns to engage donors, clients, and others.

Social Networks

Should your organization participate in social networks? There's no one-size-fits-all answer to this question. Where are your audiences now, and where are they likely to be in the future? If you can connect with them through a community they're already a part of and comfortable in, perhaps participation in social networks is worth considering.

In late 2008, the Foundation for Jewish Culture, JTA (a Jewish news agency), Jewish Educational Service of North America (JESNA), Jewish Agency for Israel, American Jewish Joint Distribution Committee, and Hillel united to create an online social network called Super Jews. Using the Facebook networks built up by these organizations' own staffers, Super Jews created a challenge that took place over the eight days of Hanukkah. Participants joined a team (red, green, or blue—much like *color war* teams from camp days) and engaged in activities online that included sharing opinions, watching video trailers, and making donations. Many participants felt they benefited from a sense of being a part of something fun, Jewish, and new. Because these organizations were trying to reach young Jews, many of whom are active Facebook users, Super Jews made perfect sense.

User-Generated Content

Increasingly, audiences expect Web sites to provide what they're looking for *and* they expect to generate content of their own by posting comments, writing reviews, listening, and being heard. Many people experienced user-generated content for the first time through Amazon.com, where people have been reviewing and rating books since the mid-1990s. In recent years, Web sites like www.yelp.com have taken this approach further, creating forums where anyone can log in; review a restaurant, hair salon, or bookstore; and comment on what others have written with no sales component or single business powering the site (sites like this generate income through advertising).

Today user-generated content is sparking serious discussions and significant shifts in many nonprofits, as they explore ways to engage in more of a two-way conversation with audiences without creating utter chaos. Organizations who've maintained message boards, chat rooms, or forums in other social media have been juggling this for years, and scrambling to react quickly and appropriately when individuals post inappropriate, damaging, or controversial content. Now these chatting communities exist on Facebook, MySpace, Bebo, Twitter, blogs, and beyond.

Here's an early example of the power of user-generated content. Epic Change, a nonprofit that uses the power of stories to create social change, used the popular social tool Twitter (www.twitter.com) over Thanksgiving 2008 to raise $11,131 in forty-eight hours to build a classroom at a school in Arusha, Tanzania. Even though the amount of money raised might not blow your socks off, the creativity and connections behind this campaign might. The campaign (detailed at www.tweetsgiving.org), invited people to participate in three easy steps. First, they were to tweet something they were thankful for out to their followers, using Twitter. Then, they were asked to make a donation at any level. Every $10 bought a brick, and 1,000 bricks equaled a new classroom. (Sound familiar? This is a classic fundraising appeal.) Epic Change would even paint a message of thanks on a person's brick, if requested. It offered the high honor of "Top Turkey" for all donors who gave $100 or more. The third and final step was to follow the Thanksgiving tweets (a *tweet* is a message sent via Twitter) of others as a way of participating in a community.

The formula behind the Tweetsgiving campaign is clear: new technology (Twitter) + relationships + donor-centric activities and premiums (sharing what one is thankful for, buying bricks) + relatable theme of gratitude = success.

Nonprofit social media visionaries such as Beth Kanter (whom I mentioned earlier in this chapter) not only helped make Tweetsgiving a success by getting the word out to their own networks (a process called *retweeting*), but they also tried their own experiments in Twitter fundraising. This campaign and others like it are reinventing the traditionally slow, often expensive process of developing traditional tools and are coming up with smart concepts wedded with social media.

Other organizations are using tools like Twitter to help individuals connect with each other and support issues they care about. The February 26, 2009, issue of the *Chronicle of Philanthropy* (Wasley, 2009) covered an event called Twestival (a compound of *Twitter* and *festival*), that raised more than $250,000 for Charity: Water in just twenty-four hours, during events that occurred in more than two hundred cities around the world.

The writing's on the wall: user-generated content is clearly here to stay. Fostering constructive two-way dialogue (rather than focusing on the old organization-centric model) is the new paradigm.

Staffing for Social Media

Other than a lack of familiarity, the biggest obstacle preventing most nonprofits from using the newer online tools is time. Setting up a Facebook page, Twitter feed, or other online community is the easy part. Generating content for it, monitoring what people are saying, and participating in the conversations that occur in these forums is truly the hard part.

Before your organization dives in, leaders and staff need to be sure it's clear who will be responsible for maintaining these new tools on a daily basis. In larger organizations, dedicated social media staff people are becoming increasingly common. In smaller organizations, a development associate, communications associate, or just a staff person who understands the tools well typically assumes responsibility. Depending on the tools you use, how active your communities are, and how robust you want the online conversation to be, maintaining these new channels will likely take somewhere between a half an hour and several hours each day.

Connecting Online with Major Donors

For the decade or so that charities have been raising money online, most of the focus has been on small gift fundraising. But in early 2008, online powerhouse Convio partnered with Sea Change Strategies and Edge Research to produce a report titled *The Wired Wealthy: Using the Internet to Connect with Your Middle and Major Donors* (download it at http://my.convio.com/?elqPURLPage=104). This report offers glimpses into the online behaviors and preferences of major and midlevel donors and reveals opportunities for nonprofits that many haven't considered yet. The report also suggests that most organizations are missing the boat when it comes to getting gifts online from major donors.

Despite evidence like this, many organizations still believe that donors won't make larger gifts online and that people over twenty-five don't use social media. My seventy-something-year-old mom might not be the most active, engaged Facebook user in the world, but she's there. Are you?

Using E-Mail to Raise Money and Inspire Action

Shortly after Sarah Palin was tapped to be John McCain's vice presidential candidate during the summer of 2008, an e-mail spread quickly online. A truly grassroots effort, this *viral* e-mail (a term used to describe something that spreads quickly on its own) was created by an unknown individual. The e-mail invited its readers to donate to Planned Parenthood in Palin's name and to request that this organization send her a card noting that a gift had been made in her honor (see Exhibit 6.1). The irony of this action wasn't lost on the Democrats and progressives who forwarded this e-mail rapidly and made donations as requested. Within a few short months, nearly $1 million was donated to Planned Parenthood as a result of this totally unplanned e-mail.

Although organizations try to start e-mail campaigns that take off like this one did, the truth is that few e-mails will go viral. To do so, they must have an original idea or piece of content that people want to share with others. They are often snarky and irreverent, or downright offensive.

EXHIBIT 6.1 This 2008 Viral E-Mail Raised Nearly
$1 Million for Planned Parenthood

Subject: Fwd: A brilliant idea for $10

Hi All:

I don't know how you feel about Planned Parenthood, but this is a great idea. I just did it myself, and feel fantastic about it. Simple, fast & cheap. And toward a great cause. Pass it along . . .

Instead of (in addition to?) us all sending around e-mails about how horrible she is, let's all make a donation to Planned Parenthood. In Sarah Palin's name. And here's the good part: when you make a donation to PP in her name, they'll send her a card telling her that the donation has been made in her honor. Here's the link to the Planned Parenthood website: https://secure.ga0.org/02/pp10000_inhonor

You'll need to fill in the address to let PP know where to send the "in Sarah Palin's honor" card. I suggest you use the address for the McCain campaign headquarters, which is:

McCain for President
1235 S. Clark Street
1st Floor
Arlington, VA 22202

P.S. Make sure you use that link above or choose the pulldown of Donate—Honorary or Memorial Donations, not the regular "Donate Online."

They're often linked with something timely or urgent such as current events or a big deadline, a reason why it's important to forward this message *now*.

Organizations that leverage e-mail effectively are using it to expand on or even replace their direct-mail programs. In 2007, Parent Project Muscular Dystrophy added a five-part e-mail series to its year-end appeal, and posted related banner ads on its Web site. The organization was already successfully raising approximately $150,000 each year from a card it mailed around Thanksgiving to current donors (called a "renewal"). By adding these e-mails that asked supporters to take other feel-good actions (such as sharing their own stories on a community site), make donations, or forward to friends, the organization raised a total of $330,000. The additional cost of producing these e-mails and banner ads was less than $15,000. In 2008, Parent Project Muscular Dystrophy repeated this approach with similarly strong results, despite the collapse of the U.S. economy.

What organizations like Parent Project Muscular Dystrophy do well is to translate the age-old practice of cultivating, asking, thanking, and stewarding donors to an online presence through copy and design that inspires action. In fact, integrating the same creative materials and approach into the Web site, e-mail, and direct mail helps ensure that the audience experiences both consistency and effective frequency.

Leveraging Online Tools Effectively

The online channel is bigger than just your organization's Web site and e-mail, and it seems to be growing it every day. Rather than get overwhelmed or ignore it, develop a manageable process to monitor what's going on and assess its relevancy to your organization's work. Here are a few suggestions to help you get started:

1. *Begin by (re)assessing your organization's Web site.* What does it say about the organization? Does it reflect the

Organizational Level and Identity Level well? Does it include current content? Does it invite conversation? Making sure this site is up to speed before you dive into other online tools or social media is an important first step.

2. *Understand which online tools your audiences use most, and how they'd like to connect with your organization.* Specifically, what social media, if any, are they already using? Are they on Facebook? Twitter? LinkedIn? (This was covered in greater depth earlier in this chapter.)

3. *Learn more about online tools and technologies—specifically, how they're being used by other organizations, what they cost, and what they take to maintain.* Most of this information can be found online. If you're not sure where to begin, Google your question. "What is Flickr?" typed into Google's search box yields a dictionary and also Wikipedia's definition, a link to Flickr .com's tour page, a link to Beth's Blog, and links to a few other places where you can start learning about Flickr, all on the first page. Younger staff people can demonstrate tools they use, and resources like Beth's Blog will help you stay on top of what's out there and how nonprofits are using them.

4. *Find someone experienced who can help your organization budget, set up, and manage social media.* Depending on how you plan to use these tools, this may mean hiring a new staff person, engaging a consultant, or perhaps working with the right volunteer. This person should also help you estimate how much time these tools will take to maintain well and figure out who should staff them on a daily basis.

5. *Plan new online activities into your workload and staff job descriptions.* Adding to or revising your communications workload in any media requires time to plan, create, set up, test, implement, and assess. Set realistic deadlines and expectations for yourself and others so that this work can happen alongside everything else on your plate. In most cases, you'll find that new online tools added to your Experiential Level don't replace other tools.

6. *Schedule activities to suit your audience's calendar.* Before you launch a new tool, particularly when resources are tight, consider when the people you hope to reach will be most receptive. If you're mailing your year-end appeal, holding a gala, and sending out an e-mail about your newest program, perhaps this isn't the month to start something new.

In Print

The most common printed communications used by non-profits are

- Annual reports
- Brochures
- Newsletters
- Direct-mail or other direct-response pieces
- Stationery
- Folders and media kits
- Flyers, postcards, or other handouts
- Posters
- Signage and banners

- Fundraising campaign materials case statements
- Event invitations, programs, and other collateral

Until recently, most nonprofits could not imagine moving away from printed materials. But today, thanks to reduced costs and the availability of broadband Internet connections, more and more organizations are heading down that path. Printed newsletters are being discarded in favor of e-mail blasts. Web sites are replacing brochures. Even annual reports are going online. Most organizations are also becoming more environmentally conscious, avoiding unnecessary printing and opting to use recycled papers and soy-based inks when possible.

But before your organization discards printing altogether, consider audience preferences and the shelf life of your documents.

Audience Preferences

Are your corporate, foundation, and key individual supporters expecting to receive a printed annual report? Are your peers' reports already on their desks? Will they give to an e-mail appeal instead of a direct-mail appeal? Similarly, are your program audiences online? What's the easiest way to inform a client in Program A about Program B?

In 2008, according to a report by the Pew Internet & American Life Project, some 55 percent of adult Americans had high-speed Internet access at home (Horrigan, 2008). But not everyone has a computer at home yet, or a high-speed Internet connection. Many organizations find that the underserved populations who are their clients are online only infrequently, or not at all.

Often, corporate philanthropy officers and major donors prefer printed materials too, perhaps for apples-to-apples comparisons, to share with other charitable decision makers, or to review at their convenience.

Printing still makes sense if you need a one-size-fits-all solution you can bring directly to people, like an overview brochure that can be distributed at conferences, street fairs, and meetings or left in the lobby.

The Direct-Mail Response Rate

For decades, direct mail has been a bread-and-butter income generator for many nonprofits. Successful direct-mail programs help organizations acquire new donors, renew existing supporters, and build awareness for their cause. However, in the past few years, a few trends have emerged that are causing many nonprofits to reconsider their direct-mail programs. First, many organizations are seeing a downward trend in response rates. The percentage that constitutes a good response rate seems to drop every few years, and is now about half of what it was when I started working with nonprofits on direct-mail projects during the 1990s. Today most organizations find they must mail a lot of pieces, have a sizable average gift size, and acquire some useful longer-term donors in order to make back their investment.

What's causing this downward trend in response rates? It may be the result of donors aging out, becoming too saturated with direct-mail appeals, or a shift in their approach to giving. Regardless of the cause of this trend, mailing appeals can seem a daunting proposition for an organization that hasn't yet built an effective direct-mail program.

Integrated campaigns (those that use e-mail and other online tools) are also shifting the direct-response landscape. Online technologies and sophisticated donor databases now allow organizations to send much more personalized messages to segments of their audiences at a very low cost.

But not all donors want to give—or even communicate—online, and direct-mail programs are still very much alive and thriving. Before abandoning direct mail, organizations should experiment with adding new channels to it (for instance, e-mail or social media) to create more three-dimensional ways for donors to connect and give.

Shelf Life

The biggest expenses in offset printing come from what printers call *makeready*: the setting up of the offset printing press. Therefore, printing more pieces reduces per-piece costs because the makeready costs are amortized over a longer print run. Extending shelf life by printing pieces in larger runs with copy that doesn't date (perhaps your organization's financials or recent program outcome metrics go on an insert, for example) can increase the returns on your investment in printing.

If a printed annual report is still necessary for your organization, consider producing it as a brochure bound within a pocket folder. Call it a *progress report* instead of annual report, and don't put a date on the cover. On the brochure pages, highlight your organization's vision, mission, values, and objectives, and use copy that integrates its key messages. Feature aspects of the organization that won't change or date quickly. Include a letter cowritten by your board chair and executive director at the front (illustrating their shared vision and collaboration.) All this content has a relatively long shelf life; it may not change for years.

Once this piece is ready to print, save it as a PDF and consider using another, more interactive tool, such as DocStoc (www.docstoc.com), ISSUU (http://issuu.com), or SCRIBD (www.scribd.com), to embed the PDF and post it to your Web site.

In the pocket of the folder for the printed version, insert pages on your organization's past year's achievements, current financials, staff and board listings, and any information customized for a particular recipient. All of this content has a relatively short shelf life; it's likely to change within a year. Printing and inserting these pages in-house allows you to keep the package up to date, and customize it for special recipients.

The Wise Giving Alliance (www.give.org) is the Better Business Bureau's charity watchdog division. In order to receive this group's seal of approval, nonprofits must meet defined criteria that include producing an annual report with a mission statement and a summary of the past year's achievements, officers, and financials. This document needs to be available to all who request it; however, there is no stipulation that it must be printed.

When your organization uses this approach, its progress report should last a minimum of two years, will meet the Wise Giving Alliance's standards, and should be a more flexible tool.

Greener Printing

Printing companies are increasingly trying to demonstrate their commitment to sustainable and responsible operations. More and more paper companies are providing fully or partially recycled paper options, for instance. Unfortunately, these papers are often more expensive than their less green counterparts. Soy- and vegetable-based inks are also more environmentally friendly options than are chemical-based inks. They are available in more vibrant colors, are easier to recycle, and are more economical in the long term. On the flip side, soy-based inks are not used by all printers and take longer to dry.

When getting estimates, always ask printers to provide you with costs for at least one recycled paper option. If they carry vegetable- or soy-based inks, ask them to price that too. Spending more for greener printing may be harder on your budget, but is likely to be more in line with your values.

In Person

In-person interactions with your organization happen when

- Visitors come to your offices for meetings.
- Clients come to facilities to participate in programs.
- Donors and the media attend events.
- Board members, staff, clients, and other people who've experienced your organization firsthand speak with their colleagues, friends, and other contacts about your agency.

The physical spaces where people experience your organization can have a profound impact on their experience but the impression these spaces create is often overlooked when offices and program spaces are built. Similarly, your organization's reputation will grow and be informed by what people are saying about their experiences with your nonprofit. However, the spaces that people visit, word-of-mouth, and your reputation among audiences are often overlooked or undervalued assets. With little expense, they can be terrific opportunities to express your organization's Organizational Level, reinforcing your credibility.

Spaces

Have you ever worked in or visited a facility that was dark, drab, or neglected? Sat in a classroom, office, or program space that felt institutional? Contrast that with spaces that are light, airy, and painted with bright colors. Every architect's and interior designer's livelihood is built on this premise: spaces have a profound impact on the people who inhabit them. Investing creativity and perhaps a little cash or elbow grease in these spaces can make a big difference in how clients and donors experience an organization.

Years ago, I volunteered with a small organization serving several local immigrant populations (most of whom spoke little or no English) in New York City. They held programs on the third floor of a run-down building, but as people entered the building's lobby, only one small sign (in English) indicated where the elevators were and what floor the agency was on. It was easy to feel lost and confused, and the drab interior of the building didn't exactly inspire confidence. One day the executive director organized a team of volunteers to paint the lobby and front door. He also installed bigger and better signs in the three languages spoken by the agency's clients. Staff created the signs and laminated them at the local copy shop, so they were inexpensive. Within days the organization appeared to be serving more people. Clients found it easier to locate the facility, which made them more comfortable recommending it to others.

Figure 6.1 shows another example—the lobby of Community Resource Exchange (www.crenyc.org). Community Resource Exchange provides strategic advice and technical services to community-based organizations that fight poverty and HIV/AIDS. Visitors to its New York City office walk into a bright, open space with café tables

FIGURE 6.1 Reception Area at Community Resource Exchange

and chairs rather than corporate-looking furniture. The words "Gathering Strength" are painted on a bright, textured wall, and information about agency services abounds. The space is often used for community meetings and events, and this design communicates CRE's personality quickly, even to the most casual visitor.

Here are a few ways you can create spaces that communicate effectively:

- Instead of choosing institutional colors and products, paint the walls and select carpeting in colors that reflect your organization's personality and are in your organization's visual identity color palette.
- Put photographs, posters, art, or signs on the walls that show your commitment to, and positive impact on, those you serve.
- Install clear signage that uses your visual identity consistently and makes it easy for people to find what they're looking for (bathrooms, conference rooms, program spaces, and so forth).
- Select comfortable furniture that inspires participation and reflects your organization's personality. For example, an agency with a *creative, eclectic* personality might use mismatched tables or chairs—perhaps hand painted—rather than generic alternatives. Selecting furniture in colors other than black, grey, or beige can also improve the way a space feels.
- Post your mission statement in communal spaces.
- Leave copies of printed communications out for visitors to pick up, read, and take.

- Have a computer available that guests can use, with your organization's Web site bookmarked as the home page.
- Staff your front desk with friendly, well-spoken people who reflect your organization's personality and are trained to make visitors feel welcomed and helped.

Do your organization's spaces feel audience-centric? Or are they designed only with economy in mind? For instance, is it clear to visitors where to go?

People

To find out whether your organization is leveraging people to communicate effectively, consider these questions:

- When asked by visitors or other interested parties, do board or staff members describe the organization consistently?
- Do people in entry-point jobs (intake staff or receptionists, for example) receive training for their positions? Do they reflect the organization's desired personality and represent it well?
- Is it easy to connect quickly with a staff person who can speak *on the record* about the organization or the issues it addresses when the press calls or a crisis emerges?

Organizations that can answer yes to these questions have effectively integrated training (discussed in depth in Chapter Five). A small investment of time and preparation up front can yield exceptional results.

Reputation

Although your organization has the ability to control many aspects of its communications, reputations are formed by a more complex set of variables. Often, they reflect authentic experiences that individuals have with your organization's programs and services, at events, or through word-of-mouth. Accurately or not, people form their own impressions about your nonprofit's work from the glimpses they catch: a quote from the executive director in an article, a scandal that wreaked havoc on another chapter of the organization, or simply what a friend said.

There are now so many media channels—television channels, online sites such as blogs, and other outlets—that media coverage doesn't raise awareness or generate donations as reliably as it once did, but it still can influence reputation. People form positive or negative associations after they read, hear, or see coverage of an organization in the newspaper, on-air news, or blog they trust. Positive coverage in the media usually builds credibility, because it's perceived as an endorsement from an objective third party.

Not sure what media coverage your organization is receiving? Tools like Google Alerts (www.google.com/alerts) can help you monitor your organization's coverage in the media by sending you e-mail alerts whenever your name or key words that you select are mentioned online.

Staying closely connected to audiences and understanding the *buzz* surrounding the organization is the most important way to monitor reputation. When your nonprofit's reputation is suffering, consider proactively developing key messages that address misconceptions and redirect perceptions.

On Air

For decades, communicating *on air* meant being on the radio or on TV. Today, with the migration of more and more communications online and onto mobile devices like phones, personal digital assistants (PDAs), and iPods, this channel is evolving. This was made clear in 2007 when Hillary Clinton and Barack Obama both announced their candidacies for president through videos posted on their Web sites. These days, audiences might experience an organization on air by

- Seeing a public service announcement (PSA) or other ad run on television, at an event, or as a trailer
- Hearing a PSA or ad on the radio
- Listening to an organization's podcast, or watching an enhanced podcast
- Watching videos on a Web site, including messages from organizational leaders, recordings of programs, and more
- Watching videos on YouTube, Vimeo, DoGooderTV (a nonprofit-oriented alternative to YouTube), or other online channels

For many years, only a handful of organizations could afford on-air communications, owing to the cost of air-time and production and a lack of staff to develop and manage these projects.

In 1986, several former advertising executives who believed that advertising is powerful enough to change behaviors and should be used to do so, founded Partnership for a Drug-Free America in order to "unsell" drugs through advertising. Since then, the partnership has relied on the pro bono creative work of major agencies like Grey Advertising, DDB Chicago, and others to develop campaigns that change the way kids view, and therefore use, drugs. For years, the ads they created ran on air for free, or were underwritten by government grants through the Office of National Drug Control Policy. Since they began, illicit drug use has dropped significantly, and use of the specific drugs targeted by the partnership's programs—including ecstasy, cocaine, heroin, and marijuana has declined (Partnership for a Drug-Free America, 2008). Nonprofits like the Ad Council have followed a similar model, working with ad agencies offering pro bono help to move perceptions around big issues. Several of the ads this collaboration produced are legendary, such as the TV ads produced for Keep America Beautiful (www.kab.org) in the early 1970s, in which Native American protagonist Iron Eyes Cody is brought to tears by littering.

Smaller organizations, especially those with less access to or experience with the world of advertising, have typically avoided investing in on-air communications, but that's starting to change. Increasingly, the low cost of shooting digital video or recording audio files (in MP3 format), coupled with free or inexpensive ways to publish them, is making it more possible than ever to use these media to move an issue.

"Overlooked: The Lives of Animals Raised for Food" is a short video produced by the Humane Society of the United States that illustrates the brutal conditions animals live in on factory farms with such force that it won DoGooderTV's 2008 video award. The Humane Society's

Web site (www.hsus.org) offers an extensive library of videos, photos, and other multimedia content generated by the organization's staff (some projects with ample production budgets, others without) and also by activists who are passionate about issues such as animal fighting, conditions at factory farms, and more. Such videos and other multimedia content exist not only on the organization's Web site, but on destinations such as YouTube, DoGooderTV, and more. The Humane Society also does an impressive job of linking its work to results through the "Victories" section of its Web site. Without a doubt, this nonprofit has identified the wired animal rights activist as its key audience online.

Organizations as well as activists are using low-cost digital production too. This strategy can be highly effective: the less professional-looking, somewhat messy quality a staff person gets when shooting his or her own video smacks of authenticity and can make a compelling case. This can be an effective strategy when *grassroots* is a defined attribute of the organization's personality.

By Mobile

Over 3.5 billion mobile phone accounts were active worldwide at the end of 2008, according to MobileActive (2009). That's more than twice the number of people who had computer-based Internet access at that time. It's estimated that 95 percent of all Americans had a mobile phone in 2008 (World Bank ICT, 2009).

"There are many people in the United States who don't have consistent Internet access, but they do have cell phones. This is particularly true for people with lower incomes, youth, and recent immigrants, for example. They're on cell phones much more than they're online," says Katrin Verclas, a leading consultant in the use of mobile phones to create social change. "If you're an organizer who wants to go where people are, consider integrating mobile messaging into your campaigns and outreach" (Katrin Verclas, personal communication, 2009). Perhaps most significant is our level of attachment to our phones: many people keep their mobile device handy 24/7: in the car, at work, at home, and by the bed while they sleep.

Most individuals throughout the world are linked by mobile phones—talking on them, text messaging (often called *SMS* or *texting*), shooting video, taking pictures, using Facebook, MySpace, and more. As of 2009, nonprofit organizations in the United States were just starting to consider how they might use mobile phones for a portion of their communications, whereas many nonprofits in Europe, Africa, and beyond have already successfully integrated mobile phones into their communications strategies. Around the world, nonprofits are now using mobile devices to get out the vote; send public messages at live events; combat tuberculosis; and provide just-in-time information about safety, the environment, corporate policies, and more. For terrific examples of who's doing what, including useful advocacy primers and other tools, visit MobileActive (www.mobileactive.org), an all-volunteer community of people and organizations using mobile phones for social impact.

In 2007, the Human Rights Campaign (www.hrc.org), which works for gay, lesbian, bisexual, and transgender equal rights, launched a mobile buyer's guide called the Corporate Equality Index, which helps you find out in real time if the store you're about to shop at supports gay and lesbian equality. Human Rights Campaign has been advising consumers on corporate equality since 2002 in print and online, but taking this service mobile was a dynamic addition that allows shoppers to access the information they want when it's most helpful. Users text "SHOP" and the name of a business to short code 30644 (a *short code* is a number you input instead of a phone number). This queries a database, which responds within seconds with a text message with the business's corporate equality rating. For example, as of April 2009, texting "SHOP Target" resulted in the following text message: "HRC awards this business a perfect 100 on our Corporate Equality Index for its strong GLBT practices & policies. Support this business." (Interestingly, Target received an 80 percent rating during the summer of 2008, which demonstrates how dynamic this tool can be.)

Because mobile is still emerging as a channel in the U.S., it remains to be seen how deeply organizations will invest in it. It's also not yet clear how responsive audiences will be to communicating with nonprofits through their phones. For now, it's viable for organizations whose programs or advocacy initiatives have time-sensitive components and audiences who are comfortable with text messaging, which seems to dominate the medium.

Fundraising by Mobile

It's early days for fundraising via mobile phone. As of this writing, only two carriers in the United States process donations via texting, and the donations are limited to $5 each. United Way pioneered *text to give* in the United States, at the 2008 Super Bowl, with a campaign that included an in-stadium component along with a TV spot that encouraged viewers to text "FIT" to "United" (864833). The campaign generated about $10,000 via text message donations from a combination of people in the stadium and television viewers. Most significantly, it demonstrated an easy way to reach new audiences and get them to give painlessly.

Preparing for the Mobile Future

Whether or not your organization is ready to plan or implement a mobile campaign, now's a good time to start collecting mobile numbers on intake and donation forms, business reply envelopes (BREs), and other points of entry. You may not be ready to text or call these individuals yet, but once you are, you'll be glad you built a list of their numbers. If that makes you nervous, remember your e-mail list: Did your organization start capturing e-mail addresses early enough? Do its databases include a high percentage of donor, member, or client e-mails? Most organizations wish they'd started gathering e-mail addresses long before they did, and have struggled to build robust e-mail lists as a result of starting late.

In Summary

- Nonprofits communicate through five channels: online, in print, in person, on air, and by mobile. These communications define the Experiential Level because these are the channels through which audiences experience a nonprofit.

- Most organizations don't have large enough communications budgets to invest in all the channels at the Experiential Level. Therefore it's important to leverage the channels and tools that are most audience-centric and that offer the biggest impact.
- The landscape is shifting at this level: social media, text messaging, and other new tools are radically altering the way people communicate. They provide opportunities for organizations to connect with donors, clients, and other audiences in innovative ways.
- If your organization isn't already collecting mobile phone numbers, it's time to start!

CHAPTER 7

Implementing Brandraising

The process of beginning brandraising at the Organizational Level, continuing to the Identity Level, and finally reaching the Experiential Level takes time. Most organizations that undertake this work start to finish find it requires a minimum of a year from the time they begin until they relaunch their new Identity in Experiential Level channels.

Moreover, as staff people shift their focus toward the big-picture questions of brandraising, day-to-day communications may feel increasingly stale and uninspiring to maintain. As the organization's visual identity and messaging platform are finalized, there's an urgent desire to use the new Identity everywhere, pronto. Because staff time and budgets are always limited in the nonprofit world, it's almost never realistic to make a wholesale change in how an organization is communicating overnight. This chapter explores how to implement and launch a new Identity and how to continue brandraising as a long-view communications strategy.

When You Can't Do It All

The older and larger an organization is, the more unrealistic it may be to make significant changes at the Organizational Level and build buy-in for brandraising. In addition, nonprofits that have been communicating for a long time typically have equity in those communications (name recognition, for instance), thus wholesale change wouldn't be a good idea (neither is change simply for change's sake). For these reasons and because of the practical reality of limited time, budget, staff, or buy-in, many organizations only partially undertake brandraising. They might integrate some of the principles of effective communication, tweak their Identity, and refine their Experiential Level, for example.

It's optimal to review the Organizational, Identity, and Experiential Levels in depth before determining what should change and what should remain the same. Ideally, a healthy exchange about the elements at each level occurs before decisions are made.

Over time, experience has shown me that some brandraising is better than none, and that even minor adjustments can yield significant results. However, the most important changes to make are often the hardest. Don't let fear of change or concern over how much work it will be dictate what your organization does or doesn't undertake. Instead, conduct an honest assessment of what will benefit your organization the most.

Relaunching Your Nonprofit's Identity

Nonprofits typically announce and reveal changes to their Identity Level communications in one of the following ways:

- *Flipping the switch.* After all core materials (Web site, brochures, stationery, templates, and so forth) have been updated, the new Identity is announced at a significant event. On that day, the new Web site goes live, and all old materials are discarded. All communications henceforth use the new Identity. This is the least confusing of the three options for staff and audiences but requires the greatest investment of time and money before launch.
- *Phased launch.* Core materials are updated as budget allows. Web site updates might be Phase 1, to be completed later. Phase 2 may involve an expanded use of social media or other interactive content, for example. Print material updates might be postponed or minimal. The new Identity is announced at an event, or informally to key stakeholders with calls or e-mail as it is rolled out. The organization has a period of transition where some old materials are still used as new pieces are introduced. Within less than a year, everything is updated and changes over.
- *Rolling launch.* As old materials run out, new materials are developed. The Web site is overhauled as time and budget allow. The period of transition is longer (and often more frustrating for staff and confusing for audiences), but thin budgets are stretched, and nothing is wasted.

To determine which approach might be best for your organization, explore the following questions:

- How much staff time and money can we allocate to the relaunch during this and next fiscal year?
- How will our audiences, particularly clients and major donors, feel about these changes? What's the best way to announce change so they buy into and support it?
- What events can be leveraged over the next eighteen months as part of the rollout? (For instance, an anniversary of the organization, launch of a new program, annual gala, and so forth.)

The faster the new Identity can be integrated, the clearer your organization's communications will be. Flipping the switch is the method most likely to inspire confidence in your audiences and avoid confusion. Phased or rolling launches are typically more common, however, because most organizations can't allocate the resources necessary to flip the switch.

Updating or Overhauling the Web Site First

For most organizations, updating the Web site so it reflects their Organizational Level and Identity Level communications clearly, using audience-centric navigation and copy, is the first major change made at the Experiential Level.

There's often resistance to making dramatic changes to the Web site after the Organizational and Identity Levels have been updated or developed. Instead, staff people often prefer to update only the visuals on the site or make only copy adjustments. Typically these "face-lift" adjustments aren't enough to effectively integrate positioning, personality, and a more audience-centric point of view. It's important to revisit the Web site's architecture, key areas, and content throughout the brandraising process. Often significant restructuring—more of an overhaul than an update—is needed to effectively integrate the Organizational and Identity Levels and new technologies and tools (for instance, social media).

Developing a Communications Plan

A *communications plan* addresses the launch of the new Identity and all external communications over a fixed period of time. I recommend that a plan cover twelve to eighteen months. Beyond that, the landscape of technology, staff capacity, budgets, and even the organization's objectives may be too variable to predict. If referred to regularly, ideally at monthly departmental or management meetings, the plan will keep everyone on the same page and link communications goals to staff capacity and budget.

Ideally, the plan will be a short, concise document that outlines how communications will be updated using the new Identity, launched publicly, and used on an ongoing basis afterward. Although many communications plans go into detail about objectives, audiences, and other Organizational Level elements, there's a risk in doing so; the plan becomes so long that it's not read or used actively. Include only the elements needed to keep people on the same page. If the plan becomes long anyway, consider breaking it into sections, ideally with the information arranged as bullet points rather than text paragraphs, so staff can refer to the items they need without too much digging.

A useful communications plan should also set the stage for your organization's new approach to communicating by linking the tools you'll use (printed brochures, social media, e-mail, and the like) with a calendar and a budget. If you're not sure where to start, begin by exploring the answers to these questions:

- Which audiences (prospective or existing donors, prospective or existing clients, the media, policymakers, and so forth) are most important for us to reach over the next twelve to eighteen months?
- Which online, on-air, in-person, in-print, or mobile communications tools are most audience-centric for us?
- Which tools will last the longest and give us the biggest bang for the buck if we develop them?
- Do these tools align with charity watchdog requirements (such as those of the Wise Giving Alliance or Charity Navigator) we might be working to achieve?
- Realistically, what's our staff capacity to create and maintain our Experiential communications?
- As ideas begin to take shape, assign a budget, deadline, and responsible party for each item.

Before you build the details of your plan into your official organizational budget and calendar, it's helpful to review the plan with staff, consultants, agencies, or others who can help your organization assess whether its budgets and deadlines reflect real-world pricing and timing for each deliverable. If you find you've budgeted too little but can't spend more, consider stretching projects out over a longer period of time (for instance, over two fiscal years) or working with freelancers and volunteers instead of consultants or agencies.

Once the plan has the support of the senior management team and includes realistic budgets and deadlines, funding must be identified or allocated. Although some organizations can fund new communications with their existing budgets, most seek grants or special gifts to cover new expenses.

Finally, convert the plan into an audience-centric schedule or calendar that will help staff to monitor the type and volume of communications each audience segment receives. Table 7.1 shows a small example of what this might look like, focusing on donor audiences.

Brandraising After Relaunch

Brandraising takes an investment of time, money, and focus that will pay an organization back many times over. In order to maximize the benefits, integrate brandraising accomplishments into the long-view culture, rather than treating the work as "something we did last year." In this section, we'll explore some of the obstacles that emerge after Identities are relaunched, and how to effectively manage Organizational, Identity, and Experiential Levels so the investment in brandraising continues to yield results.

Managing Obstacles and Change

The following events may create brandraising challenges:

- *Arrival of new board members, senior staff, or entry-point staff.* At a minimum, these individuals will need training.

TABLE 7.1 What Key Audiences Will Receive: A Partial Audience-Centric Calendar Example

	Major individual donors	Major institutional donors	Other donors
Jan	E-news	E-news	E-news
Feb			Valentine appeal
Mar	Gala	Gala	
Apr	E-news	E-news	E-news
May	Annual report drops	Foundation roundtable event Annual report drops	
June	Donor/client picnic event		Camp appeal

In some cases, they may want to make changes to the nonprofit's Organizational, Identity, or Experiential Level.

- *Significant changes in vision, mission, objectives, or values.* Any of these changes will likely require a board-level discussion about their implications for all levels of brandraising, because these Organizational Level elements are the foundations of all the work that's been developed. (These changes will probably affect most program work too.)

- *Departure of staff who championed brandraising and helped maintain it at the Identity and Experiential Levels.* If successors are found and trained quickly, this obstacle is fairly easily overcome.

- *Failure to take the long view and to integrate brandraising into communications decision making.* Staff may forget to refer to the Organizational Level elements or use the style guide. Board members may stray off message. If leadership fails to redirect them back to the brandraising framework, some of the work can unravel.

- *Negative feedback from target audiences.* Some technical feedback ("the type is too small") is easily integrated through style guide updates or changes at the Experiential Level. More significant problems might warrant refinements to the Identity Level. This is more likely to happen when audiences haven't been effectively consulted along the way.

These obstacles can be overcome through proactive planning, monitoring, and training. For example, if leadership changes, staff can proactively plan for appropriate succession internally or build a discussion about brandraising into an orientation meeting for new leadership. If people ignore or fail to use the new Identity, a brief discussion at a staff or board meeting can remind everyone of the ways in which consistency benefits the organization. Deliberate ignoring or misuse of the Identity can be addressed through one-on-one discussions between staff and their managers or between board members and the board chair. And when staff consistently receive negative feedback from audiences about particular aspects of the messaging platform or visual identity, they can share it with the director of communications (or other person responsible for managing communications) and suggest an update.

The arrival of a new executive director or powerful board member who wants to make changes without fully understanding the previous work is perhaps the hardest and most common barrier organizations face when brandraising. Before they start, send them a copy of this book and the organization's style guide. If they have questions or raise concerns, introduce them to your organization's strongest brandraising advocates (from the staff, board, and perhaps beyond) and ask them to explain how and why the work was done. They should be prepared to make a case that changes should not be made without deeper consideration and discussion. If you get your ducks in a row here, you may preempt the newcomer's desire to make change for change's sake and at the same time demonstrate your team's smarts. This may bring the added benefit of showing the new leader what a dynamic, engaged team is already in place.

A significant change in vision, mission, objectives, or values often requires making major changes in communications and elsewhere. Because these elements inform a nonprofit's positioning and personality (and all work at the Identity and Experiential Levels), changes can mean revisiting the entire scope of brandraising work. Big changes to vision and mission will usually require adjustments throughout the organization overall; it's like resetting a computer or building a new organization from scratch on the foundation of the old organization. Just as staff structure, budget, and funding sources might shift, it's likely communications will have to be adjusted too.

Avoiding a Naïve Approach

After the film *Field of Dreams* came out in 1989, people often referenced the line "If you build it, he will come." Kevin Costner's character built a baseball field in the middle of nowhere, hoping that people would somehow come out of the surrounding cornfields and make the baseball field a success. Even though today that reference is typically lost on people younger than thirty, I still love it as a way to describe a naïve approach to brandraising. Some organizations feel that "if we build it, donors will come," and so they invest little or no effort in brandraising after the Identity is relaunched. Unfortunately, it doesn't work that way. As with exercise, you have to commit to brandraising to enjoy its benefits.

Training people and having a clear style guide go a long way toward ensuring effective communications after brandraising, but these two endeavors can only go so far without a staff person committed to supporting and enforcing these efforts. Most organizations that have gone through brandraising accomplish this by designating a point person to oversee communications. Some organizations even go as far as having their staff sign a board-initiated policy stating that they'll use the Organizational and Identity Level elements consistently. Either way, the key is buy-in and enforcement.

Appointing Brand Police

Putting someone in charge of managing the Identity Level is a critical first step, ideally one that is determined before conducing training sessions. In some organizations this person is called the *brand police* or *brandraising czar*. Typically, he or she is responsible for ensuring that the new visual identity and messaging platform are used consistently and accurately. The executive director (or other chief officer) takes on this role at a smaller organization, the director of development at a midsize nonprofit (if there's no communications department), and the director of communications, external affairs, or marketing at a larger agency.

The ideal candidate for this role is someone who was involved in the brandraising process (so he or she understands the work that was done and is invested in its success) and who has a strong but likable personality. In order to be effective, this person must

- Have the authority to reject materials that may be off strategy or not accurately reflective of the Identity Level as defined in the style guide;
- Have the ability to explain why something isn't effective and to give clear directions for fixing it that

can be understood by the person doing the work (typically, a staff person, freelancer, or agency representative) without causing bigger problems (ruffling feathers, stirring up politics, and so forth);

- Have the authority to talk to leaders in order to raise issues, challenges, and new ideas that relate to any of the three Levels (Organizational, Identity, or Experiential).

The responsibilities of this person include

- Reviewing materials produced by staff to ensure that they are consistent with the Identity Level as defined in the organization's style guide
- Organizing and facilitating training sessions for new staff and board members
- Managing staff compliance with brandraising (ideally with good humor and grace)
- Notifying leaders when good reasons for revisiting or changing the Organizational, Identity, style guide, or Experiential Level come up
- Creating and implementing (or overseeing the staff who implement) a communications plan

The brand police person must bridge the gap between managing the day-to-day communications and the long view. To do this, he or she might schedule brandraising issues into the agenda of senior staff meetings once or twice each year (or more frequently, if needed). If senior staff feel that adjustments, new training, or other measures should be considered, the brand police person might also schedule these issues into board agendas and other organizational activities.

Achieving Effective Frequency Through Consistency

The advertising world coined the term *effective frequency* in the 1970s. Effective frequency refers to the number of times an individual must see or hear something before it penetrates deeply enough for this person to respond as desired (for instance, the number of times a person needs to see a car commercial before seriously considering taking a test drive at the dealership). The rule of thumb used to be that the average American must see an ad six times before actually paying attention to it. But the jury is out on what constitutes effective frequency these days, because there are more and more channels we communicate through and more and more information to process. Effective frequency for a nonprofit's messages is arguably higher than ever before.

Effective frequency is one yardstick that reminds us how difficult it is to pierce through people's defensive armor as they deflect those thousands of unwanted messages they receive every day from companies, individuals, and other nonprofits. Although it's dull work for a staff person to send out the same messages day in and day out, the recipient of those messages isn't having the same experience, because he or she isn't paying close attention.

One of the keys to getting through the clutter of communications that surrounds us all is consistency. Although it may feel tedious to work with the same visual identity and messaging platform elements every time you sit down to write or design something, it's actually a big time saver and the best way to ensure that your target audiences are receiving consistent messages from your organization. In fact, it's just about the time when most staff people feel the Identity elements are becoming tired, stale, and dull that they're starting to work.

Unfortunately, a sense of boredom with the Identity of an organization can lead to high turnover with in-house creative jobs such as designing and writing. When interviewing for these positions, ask candidates how they'll feel about working with the same elements over time, and how they'll stay fresh and creatively charged. A designer or writer who's constantly seeking to reinvent or start from scratch may not be adequately stimulated in your brandraising organization.

Integrating Brandraising into Daily Communications

Much time has been spent in this book discussing personality, positioning, long views, and other ideas that are somewhat abstract. Although all these elements can have a profound impact on how a nonprofit communicates, they have to be brought down to the day-to-day level by staff people who understand how to use them.

Using Positioning and Personality as Drivers

Just as a strong mission drives everything your nonprofit does, personality and positioning should underpin all aspects of its communications. (If you're not totally clear on what personality and positioning are and how to develop them, please refer to Chapter Four.) Here are some ways to ensure positioning and personality are effectively integrated into daily communications work:

- Staff who create or review communications work (typically, communications department staff or development staff) should consider taping a copy of the organization's positioning and personality statements above their desks so they can refer to them when writing and reviewing.
- When creating or reviewing materials, staff should constantly ask, "Does this material communicate and support our positioning? Does the design and copywriting support our personality?"

For staff who aren't communications focused, positioning and personality can be difficult concepts to understand and integrate. To make sure positioning and personality are used effectively and kept alive, communications-focused staff should work proactively to integrate them.

Keeping the Identity Level Consistent

An organization's visual identity and messaging platform (the Identity Level) are usually understood to be the turf of the communications department, although everyone in the organization should understand and use them consistently. Once an Identity is built, these elements don't usually change. In fact, one of the side benefits of having a style guide is that it captures exactly what the Identity Level is, making it perfectly clear to staff when communications have strayed off course. Day-to-day communicators can keep the visual identity and messaging platforms relevant with these strategies:

- Keep a copy of the style guide close at hand and refer to it regularly when making or reviewing online, in-print, on-air, in-person, or mobile communications.
- Keep a file that notes challenges and strengths of the Identity, and bring up these items as regular points of discussion in staff meetings. In some organizations, discussion of the Identity's strengths and challenges once or twice a year is the best way to address items that come up along the way.
- Update the style guide after any leadership-approved changes have been made to any of the elements at the Organizational or Identity Level.
- Work with other staff individually, in groups, or through training to help them understand and use the visual identity and messaging platform effectively.

Staying on Top of the Experiential Level

Most day-to-day communications occur at the Experiential Level. The Web site is updated, e-mails are sent, newsletters are written, events are held, brochures are created, and so forth. To ensure that these channels use the principles of brandraising effectively, staff people can do the following:

- *Develop communications plans targeting fundraising, program, and advocacy audiences.* Plans should be reviewed regularly and reported against at departmental and leadership meetings. They should be updated as needed and used dynamically, and not sit on a shelf passively.

- *Make sure plans are tied realistically to budgets.* There's always more communicating to do. I have yet to meet an organization that feels it has an adequate budget to communicate, no matter how large it may be. Approaching the planning process by starting with a budget and then determining how to get the biggest communications bang for your available bucks is often more effective and realistic than outlining goal projects and then cutting back if funding falls short.
- *Budget staff time, not just money, for this work.* Being clear internally who's responsible for brandraising work and making sure they have time allocated for these projects is critical.
- *Make time to pause and consider the long view.* Most staff people are understandably caught up in the never-ending stream of activities that must get done today, this week, and this month. Individually or as a department, schedule time to reflect. During an offsite retreat or a simple lunch out of the office, consider these questions:

What communications tools or trends are emerging that our organization should be thinking about now or planning for in the next fiscal year or two (social media, mobile campaigns, outreach campaigns, and so forth)?

Are they using social media? What are they doing by e-mail? How do their Web sites work? What can we learn from what they're doing? Are there any adjustments we should make to how we're communicating?

What communications skills (in writing, design, Web strategy, social media, and so forth) that we currently lack would be most useful to have in-house? Are there any conferences or workshops our staff can attend that will boost our capacity in these areas now? Should we be planning and budgeting for staff in these areas in the future?

Is our current communications plan relevant? Do we use it well? Does it need updating or a new approach to make it more useful?

These questions will help your organization anticipate and plan for the future proactively. Taking time to pause and consider them will help you avoid the trap of day-to-day reactive communications and focus on working proactively and productively.

In Summary

- There are several options for unveiling an organization's new or updated Identity, including flipping the switch, a phased launch, and a rolling launch.
- For most organizations, a Web site update or overhaul is the most critical Experiential element to address after Identity Level changes are made.
- Developing and getting buy-in for a communications plan can help staff both manage the launch of

the new Identity and shift the way communications are managed to be more audience-centric and to take a long view.

- Once a new Identity has been built, using it consistently is critical in order to fully benefit from it. Doing that takes proactive planning and management.
- Appointing and empowering someone to be the brand police is important to ensure consistent use of the new Identity.
- Anticipating challenges to brandraising and managing them head-on can minimize or negate their negative impact.
- Day-to-day communicators should keep their style guides close. Ideally, they eat, sleep, and breathe their organization's positioning, personality, visual identity, and messaging platform.
- Day-to-day communicators should get out of the trenches periodically in order to maintain perspective. Spending some time periodically to consider big-picture questions can help to eliminate last-minute surprises and communications crises downstream.

In Conclusion

Whether your organization fully implements all the principles of brandraising or bites off only a small amount, I hope you find this process valuable. Lastly, please stay in touch! I'd love to hear how brandraising works for your organization. Contact me at Sarah@bigducknyc .com, or join the conversation about brandraising at www .bigducknyc.com/blog.

ACKNOWLEDGMENTS

My husband, Craig, deserves thanks from me every day. Now they're in writing and official.

Just about all members of the staff at Big Duck during 2007 and 2008 helped by researching aspects of this book, offering great insights into what they found, refining the brandraising approach, and making it possible for me to spend time writing off site. They include Sonny Mui, Katherine Sciolto, Scott Moe, Kristen Blair, and Maria Cozine. Rebecca Hume created the snazzy *conceptual model* (and taught me what that phrase means!) that's used to illustrate the brandraising concept throughout this book. Farra Trompeter, Dan Gunderman, and Liz Brandwood were all invaluable readers and sounding boards.

Kathryn Glass is a great friend who offered smart suggestions, a keen eye, and morale support. The Boxenbaums let me use their place to write, and have really excellent tea.

My father, an author and ad man, had the words "Write, damn it, write!" framed and sitting on his desk.

That served as a good reminder of the discipline it takes to keep at it, even when it all feels uphill. Like my dad, I've benefited from much encouragement from Mindy Papp Durham—a constant muse and support.

My mother, an activist, producer, and engaged civic leader, offers daily inspiration. She taught me the importance of writing clearly when I was young and helped reinforce that in her reading of this book. Howard Ziff has helped her and me with constant cheerleading and love.

The team at Jossey-Bass was supportive, smart, and professional through-and-through.

Lastly, my sincere thanks to all the organizations that generously allowed me to use them as examples in this book. Their work is inspirational.

ABOUT THE AUTHOR

Sarah Durham is a native New Yorker who grew up in the advertising industry. She began her career in the corporate branding world, working at Hearst Publications, Prescriptive cosmetics, Disney Consumer Products, and elsewhere. In 1994, she founded Big Duck (www.bigducknyc.com), a communications firm in New York City that works exclusively with nonprofits to help them raise money and increase visibility through smart communications. Big Duck's client list includes local, regional, and national nonprofits of varying sizes. Under Sarah's leadership, Big Duck won a Presidential Design Achievement Award for its development of "Growing Up Drug-Free: A Parent's Guide to Prevention" (currently 28 million copies in circulation), and several awards from *Fundraising Success* magazine for integrated fundraising campaigns.

In 2006, Sarah was featured in *Fundraising Success* as a "Top Fundraiser Under 40." She frequently writes and contributes to articles in nonprofit trade publications. She is a volunteer trainer for the Support Center for Nonprofit Management and a frequent presenter at Association of Fundraising Professionals (AFP) conferences.

Sarah is a rabid Brooklynite, a proud mother of twin girls, and proud owner of a VW bus. She tweets about nonprofit communications under the handle "@BigDuck Sarah" and blogs at bigducknyc.com/blog. *Brandraising* is her first book.

REFERENCES

Convio, Sea Change Strategies, & Edge Research. (2008). *The wired wealthy: Using the Internet to connect with your middle and major donors*. Retrieved June 6, 2009, from http://my.convio.com/?elqPURLPage=104.

Grace, K. S., (2003). *The nonprofit board's role in setting and advancing the mission*. Washington, DC: BoardSource.

Horrigan, J. (2008, July 2). *Home broadband 2008: Adoption stalls for low-income Americans even as many broadband users opt for premium services that give them more speed*. Retrieved July 2, 2009, from http://www.pewinternet.org/Reports/2008/Home-Broadband-2008.aspx.

Kazeniac, A. (2009, February 9). *Social networks: Facebook takes over top spot, Twitter climbs*. Retrieved May 18, 2009, from http://blog.compete.com/2009/02/09/facebook-myspace-twitter-social-network.

Li, C., & Bernoff, J. (2008). *Groundswell: Winning in a world tranformed by social technologies*. Boston: Harvard Business School Press.

Lipton, M. (2003). *Guiding growth: How vision keeps companies on course*. Boston: Harvard Business School Press.

Loechner, J. (2008, April 28). *28 million mobile subscribers responded to at least one mobile ad.* Retrieved May 18, 2009, from http://www.mediapost.com/publications/?fa=Articles .showArticle&art_aid=79541.

Madden, M. (2006, April). *Internet penetration and impact.* Retrieved May 18, 2009, from http://www.pewinternet.org/ Reports/2006/Internet-Penetration-and-Impact.aspx.

Mayer, E. (n.d.). *The culture of real virtuality: The integration of electronic communication, the end of the mass audience, and the rise of interactive networks* (Discussion and summary of a chapter of *The Network Society*, Vol. 1, by Manual Castell). Retrieved May 18, 2009, from http://www.emayzine.com/infoage/ lectures/Culture_of_Real_Virtuality.htm.

MobileActive. (2009). About MobileActive.org. Retrieved June 17, 2009, from http://mobileactive.org/about.

Partnership for a Drug-Free America. (2008). *20 years of partnering with families.* Retrieved June 6, 2009, from http://www .drugfree.org/General/Articles/Article.aspx?id=cfd5a031- 7fc8-43c5-8a22-9b36eddbf72a&IsPreviewMode=true&UVer =c659fb1a-3757-488a-8b8a-9d46c9ce4ba6.

Ries, A., & Trout, J. (1980). *Positioning: The battle for your mind.* New York: McGraw-Hill.

Vargas, J. A. (2008, November 20). Obama raises half a billion online. *Washington Post.* Retrieved June 6, 2009, from http:// voices.washingtonpost.com/44/2008/11/20/obama_raised_ half_a_billion_on.html.

Wasley, P. (2009, February 26). A lesson in character development. *Chronicle of Philanthropy.* Retrieved June 6, 2009, from http:// philanthropy.com/premium/articles/v21/i09/09001301.htm.

World Bank ICT. (2009). *The Information Age (Table 5.11).* Retrieved June 16, 2009, from http://web.worldbank org/ WBSITE/EXTERNAL/DATASTATISTICS/0,,content MDK:20394827~menuPK:1192714~pagePK:64133150~piPK:6 4133175~theSitePK:239419~isCURL:Y,00.html.

INDEX

Page references followed by *fig* indicate an illustrated figure; followed by *t* indicate a table; followed by *e* indicate an exhibit.

National Brain Tumor Society's example of, 99e-100

Brand police, 162-164

Branding: accidental, 14-16; examining the nonprofit applications of, 1-3

Brandraising: as communication framework, 4-5; description and meanings of, 3-5; Experiential Level of, 33, 35, 60-61, 111-148; following the Identity relaunch, 157, 159-165; Identity Level of, 32-33, 34-35; implementing, 151-170; integrating into daily communications, 165-169; measuring and assessing impact of, 35-37; Organizational Level of, 31-32, 34, 41-70; quantitative and qualitative metrics of, 37-38

Brandraising czar, 162-164

Brooklyn Botanic Garden, 48

Brooklyn Community Foundation, 90

Budgets: communication plans tied to, 168; for staff time, 168; for upgrading your organization Web site, 25-26

C

Celebrity training, 108-109

Charity: Water's Twestival event, 126

Chronicle of Philanthropy (magazine), 126

Clients: how they experience your organization, 114-116; offering special services to accommodate, 116

Clinton, H., 143

CMYK color system, 84, 85

Colloquial usage, 92-94

Color processes: description and types of, 84-85; linking sub-brands to main Identity using, 103-104fig

Common Craft, 121

Communications: brandraising as framework for, 4-5; how objectives shape, 53-54; Identity Level, 153-161; integrating brandraising into daily, 165-169; key messages of, 89, 97-98, 99e; measuring the value of, 5-7; Organizational Level day-to-day, 67-68; positioning and personality as drivers of, 165-166; principles of effective, 9-29; staying on top of Experiential Level, 167-169; underwriting changes for nonprofit, 27-28. *See also* Marketing

Communications obstacles: Barriers to Effective Communications survey (2008) on, 9-10; managing Identity Level, 157, 159-161; three greatest, 10

Society's example of, 100e–101
Epic Change, 125–126
Experiential Brandraising Level: on air communications used at the, 143–145; in-person communications used at the, 137–142; leadership involvement at the, 35; mobile communications used at the, 145–148; online channels used during the, 120–132; overview of, 33–34, 111–112; using positioning to measure communication of, 60–61; printed communications used at the, 132–137; selecting audience-centric channels at the, 112–120; staying on top of communications at the, 167–169

F

Facebook, 17, 18, 121, 125, 128, 131
Feel-good, 22–23
Field of Dreams (film), 161
Flickr, 25, 121, 131
For-profit organizations: branding value for, 2; transactions by, 7. *See also* Nonprofit organizations
Foundation for Jewish Camp: Community by the Cabinful, 92
Foundation for Jewish Culture, 124
FrontPage, 25

Fundraising: communications plans targeting, 167–168; Epic Change's use of Twitter for, 125–126; leveraging e-mail for, 129–130; mobile communication channel use for, 147–148; viral e-mail used for, 128
Fundraising audiences, 55
Furlong, P., 45

G

Gaining perspective, 23–24
Generation Ys (Millennials), 20
GIF format, 83
Gill Sans, 83
Google, 17
Google Alerts, 142
Google logo, 76*fig*
Grace, K. S., 44
Graphic decorative elements, 85
Grassroots personality, 145
Greener printing trend, 137
Grey Advertising, 144
Groundswell: Winning in a World Transformed by Social Technologies (Li and Bernoff), 122
GuideStar, 113
Guiding Growth: How Vision Keeps Companies on Course (Lipton), 43

H

Helvetica (film), 80
Helvetica typeface, 83
Hex color system, 84–85

Information saturation management, 16–18
InMail, 17
Internet use survey (2006), 17
Iron Eyes Cody, 144
ISSUU, 136

J

Jewish Agency for Israel, 124
Jewish Educational Service of North America (JESNA), 124
Johnson & Johnson, 60
JPEG format, 83
JTA (a Jewish news agency), 124

K

Kanter, B., 122, 126
Kazeniac, A., 17
Keep America Beautiful, 144
Key messages: description of, 89, 97; how to develop and use, 98; National Brain Tumor Society examples of, 97–98, 99e

L

Leadership: brandraising role of, 34–35; Identity integration training for, 106–107; managing Identity relaunch changes and obstacles among, 157–161; role in defining organizational values, 51–52
Lexicon: description and function of, 89, 101;

Osborne Association's example of, 101, 102e
Li, C., 122
LinkedIn, 18, 121, 131
Lipton, M., 43
Loechner, J., 17
Logos: BAM, 76fig; choosing the right kind of, 79–80; definition and types of, 75–76; Google, 76fig; with icons or marks, 76, 77–78; linking sub-brands to main Identity using, 103–104fig; logotypes and acronyms, 76, 78–79; redesigns: before and after, 81fig
Logotypes, 76, 78–79
Long view perspective: accidental branding, 14–16; assessing your organization's, 13t; benefits of seeing the, 10–12; making time to consider the, 168; managing information saturation for, 16–18; monitoring the landscape for, 16; reinforcing the big idea, 18–19, 32, 59–62; working reactively, 12. See also Short view perspective

M

Madden, M., 17
Makeready costs, 135
Managing information saturation, 16–18
March of Dimes, 46, 60, 77

Office of National Drug Control Policy, 144

On air communication channels: advertising form of, 143–144; examples of, 143; low-cost digital video productions as, 144–145

Online communication channels: connecting online with major donors, 127–128; using e-mail to raise money and inspire action, 128–130; getting into Web 2.0, 120–127; leveraging online tools effectively, 130–132; listed, 120

Opportunity Agenda, 49–50e

Organization culture: values of, 32, 49–52, 159, 161; vision and, 32, 42–44, 96–97, 159, 161; working reactivity, 12. *See also* Mission

Organizational Brandraising Level: audiences element of, 32, 55–59; foundation for everyday activities at the, 66–70; in-person communications which express the, 137–142; integrating Identity and, 154–155; leadership involvement at the, 34; mission element of, 32, 44–49, 61–62, 96–97, 159, 161; objectives element of, 32, 52–56, 159; overview of, 31–32; personality element of, 32, 62–66, 79, 85, 123, 140,

145, 165–166; positioning element of, 32, 47, 59–62, 165–166; qualitative and quantitative metrics of, 37–38; strategic planning, 42; values element of, 32, 49–52, 159, 161; vision element of, 32, 42–44, 96–97, 159, 161; visual Identity reflecting attributes of, 33, 75–87*fig*

Organizational Brandraising Level activities: getting ready to begin brandraising, 68–70; informing day-to-day communications, 67–68; overview of, 66–67

Organizational Brandraising Level mission: crafting the mission statement of, 46–49; definition of, 32; development of effective, 44–46; revising, 46

Osborne Association, 101, 102e

"Overlooked: The Lives of Animals Raised for Food" (video), 144–145

P

Palin, S., 128, 129e

Parent Project Muscular Dystrophy: connecting audiences with objectives, 56; e-mail fundraising campaign by, 129–130; mission of, 45–46;

objectives of, 53e, 54; social networking used by, 54. *See also* Duchenne muscular dystrophy

Partnership for a Drug-Free America, 90, 143–144

Personality: Apple Computer ad campaign use of, 62–63; communication context of, 32, 62–63; as communication driver, 165–166; distinguishing your organization through, 65–66; effective use of space reflecting, 140; graphic elements communicating, 85; grassroots, 145; how to communicate, 63–64; in-house definition of, 64–65; selecting logo that reflects, 79; using state of the art media reflecting on, 123

PETA, 79

Pew Internet & American Life Project, 133

Photographs, 85

PhotoShop, 86

Planned Parenthood, 128–129e

PMS (Pantone Matching System), 84, 85

Podcasting, 122

Point-of-entry staff, 108

Points of entry, 113–114

Policymakers, 117–118

Polio, 46

Positioning: The Battle for Your Mind (Ries and Trout), 59

Positioning: as communication driver, 165–166; comparing mission to, 61–62; description of, 32, 59; how to use, 60–61; in-house defining of, 62; mission statement which help, 47

Positioning statements, 60

Printed communications: audience preferences for, 133–134; direct-mail response rate, 134–135; greener printing trend of, 137; makeready expense of, 135; most commonly used, 132–133; shelf life of, 135–136

Program audiences, 55

Prospects. *See* Donors (or prospects)

Public service announcement (PSA), 143

R

Red Crescent icon, 78

Red Cross, 60, 76, 77fig, 78

Reinforcing big idea, 18–19

Reputation, 142

Retweeting, 126

RGB color system, 84–85

Ries, A., 59

Robin Hood Foundation: Targeting Poverty in New York City, 92

ROI (return on investment): measuring value of communications, 5–7; profit measurement of, 5

S

Safe Horizon, 90, 91*t*
Save the Children, 90
Science (magazine), 23
SCRIBD, 136
Sea Change Strategies, 127
Serif typeface, 82
Short view perspective, 13*t*. *See also* Long view perspective
Slow Food USA, 48
Social bookmarking, 122
Social marketing campaigns: effective, 38; viral e-mail format of, 128–129*e*
Social media: assessing your use of, 168–169; effectively leveraging, 130–132; learning to use, 120–122; relevance for your nonprofit, 122–123; staffing for, 127; user-generated content for, 124–126. *See also* Media; Technology
Social networking: description of, 25; Facebook for, 17, 18, 121, 125, 128, 131; fundraising through, 125–126; LinkedIn for, 18, 121, 131; organizational participation in, 124; Parent Project Muscular Dystrophy community, 54; Super Jews, 124; Twitter, 121, 122, 125–126, 131. *See also* Media; Web 2.0
Space: Community Resource Exchange reception area and, 139*fig*–140; in-person communication impact by, 138–140; tips on creating effective, 140–141; which reflects personality, 140
Staff: appointing brand police or brandraising czar among, 162–164; brandraising benefits to, 35–36, 38; budgeting for time of, 168; gaining perspective, 23–24; Identity integration training for, 106–107; improving communications skills of, 169; lack of professional communications, 26–27; managing departure of brandraising champions among, 159; managing Identity relaunch changes and obstacles among, 157–161; point-of-entry, 108; using positioning and personality as drivers, 165–166; role in defining organizational values, 51; social media responsibilities of, 127
Staff spokespeople, 108
Strategic planning: objectives defined through, 32, 52–55; Organizational Brandraising Level, 42
Style guide: description of, 104–105; elements and functions of, 105–106
Sub-brands: description and function of, 103; linking main Identity to, 104*fig*

96–97; Organizational Level of Brandraising role of, 32, 42–44

Vision statements, 43

Visual Identity platform: color, 84–85; description of, 33, 75; logos, 75–80, 81*fig*; mood boards, 85–87*fig*; photographs, icons, other graphic elements, 85; typography, 80, 82–84

W

Warm fuzzy, 23

Web 2.0: learning to use, 120–122; relevance for your nonprofit, 122–123; staffing for social media, 127; user-generated content using, 124–126. *See also* Social networking

Web sites: ASPCA, 21; "Beth's Blog: How Nonprofits Can Use Social Media," 122; Betty Ford Center, 48; Big Duck, 170; Brooklyn Botanic Garden, 48; Common Craft, 121; Community Resource Exchange (CRE), 139; DocStoc, 136; Google Alerts, 142; Human Rights Campaign, 146; Human Society of the United States, 145; ISSUU, 136; Keep America Beautiful, 144; Li and Bernoff's blog, 122; NTEN: The Nonpofit Technology Network, 122;

NTEN's We Are Media project, 122; Parent Project Muscular Dystrophy, 45, 54; SCRIBD, 136; Slow Food USA, 48; Survey Monkey, 112; Taproot Foundation, 101–102; Twitter, 125; typography used for, 82–84; user-generated content of, 124–126; *The Wired Wealthy: Using the Internet to Connect with Your Middle and Major Donors* report, 127–128; Wise Giving Alliance, 136; www .yelp.com, 125; Zoomerang, 112–113. *See also* Nonprofit organization Web sites; Technology

The Wired Wealthy: Using the Internet to Connect with Your Middle and Major Donors report, 127–128

Wise Giving Alliance, 113, 136

Women's Sports Foundation logo, 81*fig*

Working reactivity, 12

World Bank ICT, 145

World Wildlife Federation, 77

Written brand, 88. *See also* Messaging platform

www.yelp.com, 125

Y

YouTube, 25, 121, 143, 145

Z

Zoomerang, 112–113